Industrial Democracy in Europe Revisited

INDUSTRIAL DEMOCRACY
IN EUROPE
REVISITED

Industrial Democracy in Europe (IDE)
International Research Group

OXFORD UNIVERSITY PRESS
1993

Oxford University Press, Walton Street, Oxford OX2 6DP
Oxford New York Toronto
Delhi Bombay Calcutta Madras Karachi
Kuala Lumpur Singapore Hong Kong Tokyo
Nairobi Dar es Salaam Cape Town
Melbourne Auckland Madrid
and associated companies in
Berlin Ibadan

Oxford is a trade mark of Oxford University Press

Published in the United States
by Oxford University Press Inc., New York

British Library Cataloguing in Publication Data
Data available

Library of Congress Cataloging in Publication Data
Industrial Democracy in Europe. International Research Group.
Industrial democracy in Europe revisited / by Industrial Democracy
in Europe (IDE), International Research Group.
Includes bibliographical references.
1. Industrial management—Europe—Employee participation.
I. Title.
HD5660.E915 1993 331'.01'12094—dc20 92–41446
ISBN 0–19–828786–0

Typeset by Pure Tech Corporation, Pondicherry, India
Printed in Great Britain
on acid-free paper by
Biddles Ltd.
Guildford and King's Lynn

To Oiva Laaksonen and Eliezer Rosenstein

Both unforgotten as friends, always admired as colleagues

After two hours I shall sail away
to a three weeks' summer-holiday

Oiva Laaksonen's last sentence in a letter of 16 July 1989 commenting on a draft on this book. On 26 July 1989 he died in an accident aboard his sailing-boat.

Eliezer Rosenstein died suddenly on 27 November 1991 while still finalizing the draft of the most important chapter, Chapter 2 of this volume.

Preface

This study of Industrial Democracy in Europe (IDE) is an international collaborative effort to assess the effects of national schemes for employee participation on a comparative basis. The co-operation of IDE network of some thirty colleagues from fourteen countries covers two decades. The empirical research took place in two stages: Industrial Democracy in Europe I (IDE I) in 1975/7 and Industrial Democracy in Europe II (IDE II) in 1986/7.[1] Results of the first stage were published in two volumes by Oxford University Press: *Industrial Democracy in Europe* (1981) and *European Industrial Relations* (1981).

The present volume reports the findings of the second study, which is now called: 'Industrial Democracy in Europe Revisited'. The book describes the second study and compares its findings with the research carried out ten years earlier. This two-phase longitudinal study with data collections ten years apart was carried out in the same establishments. The focus of the book is, therefore, empirical rather than policy-oriented. As such it is shaped by the original data set and the time-frame of our research (1976–86). Of course, there have been many important policy developments since that time, particularly those associated with the Social Charter in the EC countries which are not covered in this book. Furthermore, there have been important, sometimes dramatic, political developments after 1986 which literally redesigned the political map of Europe and/or reversed the traditional political order in a given country. This is particularly true for three countries included in this IDE II study: Yugoslavia, Poland, and Germany. These political events occurred after our research although precursors of them could be noted already during the decade covered by our research. Rather than trying to pursue the futile attempt to document such ongoing political developments we focus our report on the decade which is marked by two points in time separating our two waves of empirical research: 1977 and 1987.

The IDE International Research Group could not have carried out the task of a second research phase without the support of the Volkswagen Foundation (Hanover), the Maison des Sciences de l'Homme (Paris), and the Danish Research Foundation, who have with their support facilitated the international co-operation of the IDE International Research Group, the requisite data documentation and analysis, and—last

[1] When referring to the period between the two measurement points in time we will henceforth use 1977/87, for brevity's sake.

but not least—the preparation of the manuscript for this volume. We gratefully acknowledge their critical assistance.

However, we also have to thank a large set of national and international funding agencies:

Belgium	Seminarie en Laboratorium voor Sociopsychologie van het Bedrijfsleven, Rijksuniversiteit Gent
Germany	Anglo-German Foundation, Volkswagen Stiftung
Israel	Fund for the promotion of Research at the Technion (VPR)—Israel Institute of Technology
Netherlands	Netherlands Organization for Scientific Research (NWO)
Norway	Norwegian Research Council for Applied Social Science (NORAS)
UK	Anglo-German Foundation
Yugoslavia	National Research Foundation of Slovenia, Ljubljana
Poland	Technical University Radom

The products of the IDE International Research Group result from a collective enterprise. Each member's inputs were necessary conditions for the success of the joint venture. It is impossible to do justice to all individual contributions, to each idea generated, each improving critique provided by a member of the IDE Group, or by a national team. Hence, the collective authorship. However, it is necessary to recognize and acknowledge especially critical inputs into the collective work of the IDE International Research Group. First, Peter Bott for his devotion and efforts in data handling. Several members of the IDE International Research Group served in a 'Committee of Chapter Drafters'. It was their task to provide (often several) drafts of the chapters in this book to the whole IDE Team for improvements and critical comments. Bernhard Wilpert for Chapter 1. Eliezer Rosenstein for Chapter 2 which necessitated a wide range of secondary data analysis. It was mainly prepared while being a fellow at the Netherlands Institute for Advanced Studies (NIAS). We are thankful to NIAS for having provided this opportunity. Pieter Drenth for Chapter 3. Riccardo Peccei for Chapter 4 which involved considerable additional data analyses and refinements of theoretical argumentation. Frank Heller and Malcolm Warner for Chapter 5. Support from the Maison des Sciences de l'Homme enabled the Committee of Chapter Drafters to meet in Paris in October 1990 to do the necessary work for finalizing the manuscripts for this volume.

Factual information concerning individual countries was provided by the respective country teams (see list below) who take responsibility for their validity.

The IDE International Research Group would very much like to thank Bernhard Wilpert for his distinctive leadership in promoting the project through its initial, and then later phases, a period of nearly two decades. All the group would keenly support this accolade: without him the ship would have been rudderless.

THE IDE INTERNATIONAL RESEARCH GROUP

The IDE Group consists of the team members that were part of IDE I and of those who joined for IDE II (asterisked):

Belgium	Rie Claes*, Pol Coetsier, Marnix Ryckaert
Denmark	Flemming Agersnap
Finland	Oiva Laaksonen
France	Dominique Martin, Janine Goetschy
Germany	Peter Bott*, Jörg Rayley, Bernhard Wilpert
Italy	Francesco Consoli, Titta Vadalá, Riccardo Peccei
Israel	Eliezer Rosenstein
Japan	Akihiro Ishikawa*, Koji Okubayashi*
Netherlands	Erik Andriessen, Pieter J. D. Drenth, Cornelis Lammers, Paul Koopman*
Norway	Thoralf Qvale, Ragnvald Kalleberg*, William Lafferty*
Poland	Anatol Peretiatkowicz
Sweden	Thomas Sandberg, Bengt Stymne
UK	Peter Abell, Frank A. Heller, Malcolm Warner
Yugoslavia	Vesna Pusić, Veljko Rus.

Corresponding Members

Walter Goldberg, Theo Pirker, Stanley Seashore, William H. Starbuck.

Associate Researchers

Gabriele Freidank (Germany); Itzhak Gur-Lavie (Israel); Wolfgang Potrats (Germany); Malcolm Wilder (Great Britain); Svein Hovde* (Norway); Darinka Vrecko* (Yugoslavia); Eli Maissis* (Israel); Avraham Ofek* (Israel); Jeroen Pool (Netherlands); Birthe Skov Pedersen* (Denmark).

International Coordination

Bernhard Wilpert.

The IDE International Research Group
January 1992

Contents

List of Figures

List of Tables

1

Introduction to an International Comparative Replication Study

RATIONALE

Replication studies in the social sciences are a rare event: they are costly; they require repeated access to research sites; they demand the sustained interest and motivation of researchers over extended periods. No wonder then that international comparative replications of organization studies are seldom carried out (exceptions: Kern and Schumann 1984; Heller *et al.* 1987). There is a further deterring reason: the complexities of maintaining the co-operation of a large research team against the odds of long-distance communication, different time-schedules, lack of resources for international collaboration, the fear that replications might show deficiencies in earlier studies. However, this study tells the story of such a rare realization.

In 1975/6, the *Industrial Democracy in Europe International Research Group* conducted an investigation in ten West-European countries, Israel, and Yugoslavia on the impact of formal rules and regulations upon participation within enterprises (IDE 1981*a*; 1981*b*). Altogether 134 establishments, matched according to size and technology, contributed to the research which included semi-structured interviews with close to 1,000 key respondents and a questionnaire study of about 8,000 randomly selected employees in the 134 establishments. Let's call it the IDE I study. This book reports on IDE II, a replication '10 years after' (more specifically: in 1986/7), while using the results of IDE I as a point of comparison.

Many things may have changed in the twelve IDE countries[1] within a period of ten years. A decade is a long time in the life of an enterprise, as well as in the macro-contexts which may affect their day-to-day conduct and operations, e.g. participation. Such presumed changes refer to their economic situation, their technological advancement, the industrial relations system, their political climate, and work-related values and expectations. The economic crisis of the late 70s and early 80s has

---

[1] IDE I countries were Belgium, Denmark, Finland, France, Italy, Israel, Netherlands, Norway, Sweden, UK, West Germany, Yugoslavia.

brought troubling unemployment figures to most IDE countries which affects employment opportunities and hence, possibly, negotiating and bargaining power of employees and their unions. While experts still debate to what degree the introduction of new information technologies impacts on the availability of jobs (Dostal 1982), one thing is very likely: technological change and the adequate use of new techniques imply changing qualification demands (Stoob 1985) which may set new constraints and opportunities for worker autonomy and intra-organizational decision-making (Dirrheimer and & Wilpert 1983). Furthermore, some countries have changed their political complexion by bringing new governments to power that may be both facilitating or impeding the voice of employees in their work organization. New legislation has thus brought changes to the national industrial relations systems in Finland, France, the Netherlands, Norway, Sweden, and the United Kingdom. Similarly, governmental programmes to improve the quality of working conditions may serve as examples of such changes on the national level, the huge German 'Humanization of Work Programme' (more recently: 'Technology and Work Programme') being a case in point (Wilpert and Ruiz Quintanilla 1984). Finally, socio-cultural changes in work-related value patterns have been interpreted as inducing higher aspiration levels for workers in terms of involvement in organizational decisions of their concern. Schematically, the impact of these changes may be depicted as in Figure 1.1. Not all these complex factors can easily be measured with available statistics, but the broad systems level picture should be borne in mind when assessing the total situation.

Speaking on the most general level, the purpose of replication studies in the area of industrial democracy is threefold:

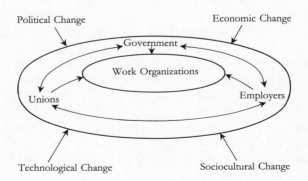

Fig. 1.1 Influence Patterns in Industrial Relations

1. To ascertain whether the major findings of the original study of time 1 (t1) can be demonstrated to hold at time t2. In that sense a replication facilitates a test of robustness of the empirical findings over time and, hence, a confirmation of their theoretical and practical significance.
2. To provide the possibility to measure changes that may have occurred in important domains of the phenomena studied.
3. To arrive at statements about the causal direction and outcomes of such changes.

These three reasons provide a general basis for IDE II. The more specific objectives of the replication will be outlined below in the context of the history of the IDE research as a whole.

THE DEVELOPMENT OF IDE RESEARCH

IDE I

IDE I developed out of discussions among interested participants at the First International Sociological Conference on Participation and Self Management, in Dubrovnik in 1972. A series of research workshops (for details see IDE 1981*a*: ch. 3) finally resulted in the formation of a large international interdisciplinary research team which agreed to carry out a concerted research effort in twelve countries. The research was described to be 'decentralized-collective' and the modalities of the co-operation were outlined in a 'social contract' (Drenth and Wilpert 1980). Decentralization implies responsibility of each national team for funding the conduct of the national sub-study and interpretation of national findings. 'Collective' connotes sharing of theoretical and methodological developments of all international data, of authorship, and of international overheads to facilitate meetings, standardization, and co-ordination. As it was phrased in IDE 1981 (p. 3):

The project required the merging of a variety of interests in industrial democracy which included political and philosophical interests; interests relating to social science theory; methodological interests; interests arising out of ongoing or past research; and practical needs and interests. Very quickly, however, the main focus of the research was established—the differential distribution of power and influence in organizations subject to different types of national industrial democracy schemes. Recent developments in industrial democracy have been preoccupied with formal rule-making and the research was designed to establish if changes in positive law have, and can, bring about changes in structure and behaviour, and what conditions make for the success or failure of legislation to increase worker participation.

The core theoretical model of the variables that were measured in IDE I postulated a relationship between formal rules for participation

(Participative Structure—PS), the distribution of influence and participation in companies (Power—Po), organizational context factors (Con) as moderators or co-predictors of Po, and a set of attitudinal outcomes (O) (see Figure 1.2). The methodological approach of IDE I employed a wide variety of data collection techniques which included document analyses (laws, collective agreements, organizational materials), semi-structured interviews of key informants (N = 997), from the establishments (N = 134), and a questionnaire survey among randomly selected employees (N = 7832) from the 134 establishments. The *national context* of twelve participating countries was taken as a natural experimental setting. These national contexts were described qualitatively on the basis of a common framework which led to a separate publication (IDE 1981*b*). What follows is a brief description of the major features of the methods employed. They are described here only in so far as they are relevant for or significantly different from the instruments used in IDE II (for details see IDE 1981*a*: ch. 4).

The interview and questionnaire procedures partly relied on available instruments (e.g. organizational measures developed by researchers, known as the Aston school, Pugh and Hickson 1976), partly by the IDE team itself. On the whole these techniques followed classical paths of organizational research. However, new ground was broken by developing methods of systematically measuring norms and rules for participation, thus facilitating for the first time the possibility to relate *Participative Structures* (PS) systematically to measures taken at the level of the organization and the individual. PS, by virtue of being predominantly legislative or collective norms, can be viewed as mainly belonging to the institutional or meso-level. In other words, to relate such meso-level data systematically to micro-level data on the organizational or individual level constituted a major methodological breakthrough in comparative organization research.

Specifically, PS refer to the formal, written-down framework of participation in organizations. It may be based on national laws, bargaining contracts, or managerial policies. Thus, it refers to formal operative rules

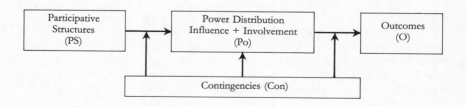

Fig. 1.2 Theoretical Core Model of IDE I

and regulations for the intensity of participation of various parties (bargaining groups) in organizational decision-making.

As *bargaining groups* IDE I identified the following categories (IDE 1981*a*: 51–2):

A Workers, white- and blue-collar, without supervisory functions.

B First-line supervisors, foremen (lowest level of supervisory functions).

C Middle managers: according to establishment usage; all hierarchical levels above B and below D (including staff members at comparable levels).

D Top management: according to establishment usage all persons considered to belong to the top management of the establishment.

E Level above the plant: control or supervisory groups, managerial bodies (e.g. conglomerate management), shareholders, or owners.

F Permanent representative bodies at the establishment level, no matter of what origin: works' councils, workers' councils, union representative bodies, and union representatives like shop stewards.

G Bodies/institutions outside the company, external groups (not necessarily outside the establishment): unions, banks, community councils, regional planning councils, etc.

The intensity of prescribed participation was ascertained on the basis of a set of sixteen decisions (Fig. 1.3). Document analyses (of laws, collective agreements, managerial policies) then enabled the researchers

Time perspective	Content of decisions		
	Work/social conditions	Personnel	Economic aspects
Short-term	Task assignment Personal equipment Working conditions Working hours Holidays	Training courses Transfers	
Medium-term	Work study Wage levels	Dismissals Hiring procedures New department head Appointment own supervisor	Reorganization
Long-term			Investment New product

Fig. 1.3 Decision-set Paradigm

to identify each bargaining group's prescribed participation (Mode of
Participation) in each of the sixteen decisions with the help of a specific
scale:

1   No regulations.
2   Information (unspecified) must be given to the group.
3   Information *ex ante* must be given to the group (i.e. before the
    decision is made).
4   Consultation of the group is obligatory (i.e. group must always be
    consulted prior to the decisions taken).
5   Joint decision-making with the group (i.e. group has the power of
    veto and must give its approval).
6   Group itself has the final say.

The *Power Distribution* (PO) in IDE I was measured by an *Influence*
measure (PO1) and a measure of *Involvement* (PO2). Key informants
(N = 997) from management and unions judged the influence of each of
the seven Bargaining Groups in each of the sixteen decisions with the
help of a five-point scale, ranging from 'no influence' to 'very much
influence'. The differential *de facto* and desired *Involvement* (PO2) of
employees in making the sixteen decisions was obtained from a questionnaire survey of 7,832 employees randomly selected from the participating establishments. The Involvement Scale consisted of basically the
same six steps as the ones in the scale used for Participative Structure
(1 = 'I am not involved' . . . 6 = 'I decide on my own'). The Outcomes (O)
were attitudinal and evaluative measures concerning organizational climate, participation, and satisfaction.

The choice of the 134 establishments included in IDE I was made on
the basis of size and industrial sector in order to achieve a maximum of
comparability among the organizations under study. It was mainly features such as technology, organizational structure, personnel structure,
and certain financial and economic features of the establishments that
formed the contingency variables in the research of IDE I. The measurements were largely identical or derived from the instruments of the
Aston School.

The major results of the IDE I study were to demonstrate that:

- *de facto* participation and desired participation of employees in the
  establishments studied were generally rather low (exception:
  Yugoslav establishments);
- positive effects of hierarchy on participation levels could univer-
  sally be noted, irrespective of societal context and economic system;
- size and technology of establishments had little or no impact on *de
  facto* participation;

- participation systems with relatively high degrees of formalization (e.g. Yugoslavia, Germany) were evaluated significantly more positively by employees than were systems with lower degrees of formalization;
- the best predictors of *de facto* participation were indeed rules and regulations (PS) combined with certain organizational context factors, notably employee mobilization and leadership style (for details see IDE 1981*a*).

IDE II

The IDE International Research Group had continued over the years to meet periodically to discuss current research interests while using some of the collective royalties that went to a non-profit association under German law (the 'IDE Fund' specifically formed by the IDE team for that purpose). In 1983, again at a plenary meeting in Dubrovnik, it was decided to conduct a replication in the mid-80s in the very same establishments that had been studied in the mid-70s.

A series of subsequent meetings in 1983 and 1984 elaborated and refined the research strategy. Only a subset of the same measures were to be used and the replication (due to cost considerations) was to *be confined to key senior management and union respondents alone* and so, therefore, the measurement of influence. Basically the same theoretical model, the same categorization of bargaining groups, and the same set of sixteen decisions were to underly the replication as its predecessor. However, it had to be expanded and restricted at the same time. The restriction was necessary because of the decision to forego another survey of randomly chosen employees and the measurement of personal involvement. The expansion was advised because the major motive for the replication was the challenge and opportunity also to include changes in the macro-context:

- In the mid-70s, few in the international team and among the consulted practitioners considered new technologies as a major determining issue. In the mid-80s, it shaped public discourse. Hence, the additional decisions on technological innovation were added to the set of sixteen decisions essential to be quoted in the qualitative description of country contexts.
- In the mid-70s unemployment figures were not even deemed to be central in the qualitative description of country contexts. In the mid-80s they were of central political concern everywhere. Hence, we collected data on labour-market situations and labour (see Questionnaire in Appendix C).
- In the mid-70s the debate about materialist and post-materialist values (Inglehart 1977) had hardly begun: in the mid-80s, it was in

full swing. We tried to include some measures on value changes in the different IDE countries but failed due to lacking comparable databases.

Furthermore, during the decade in question some countries introduced major legislative changes to affect participation (Finland, Sweden, France). This presented a unique opportunity to study the robustness of one of the main findings of IDE I: the impact of externally induced organizational change, i.e. the impact of rule making on *de facto* participation.

In view of these macro factors (MAC) and the self-inflicted restrictions on the research design described above the research model of IDE II was designed to be as in Figure 1.4. The aspirations of IDE II are clear: based on the data from IDE I, and with the inclusion in IDE II of MACro-measures it is the intention to elucidate the dynamic impact and interaction of macro and meso as well as organizational context measures in their influence on *de facto* participation. If successful, this strategy will help to advance the theoretical understanding of industrial democracy by interrelating for the first time systematically macro-, meso-, and micro-level data from two measurements made ten years apart. The IDE research, without prior reflection, intention, or planning, had turned from a cross-sectional study into a longitudinal panel research with the establishments of IDE I as its panel members. As such it shares all the bedevilling problems of all longitudinal research (Schaie and Herzog 1982), i.e. those of instrumentation (intermittant changes in research methods used), statistical regression (unreliable data tend to regress towards the mean), mortality (attrition of cases from one measurement to the next), changing population (the population from which the study's sample was drawn may have changed between measures which reduces the external validity of results), number of measurement points (two points are often insufficient to discriminate general trends from haphazard oscillations). In addition to these methodological queries IDE II was faced with a host of practical problems.

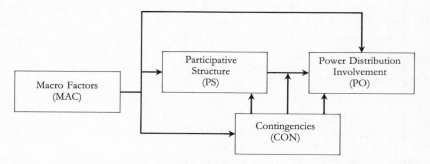

Fig. 1.4 Theoretical Core Model of IDE II

At this point it must suffice to take but a cursory look at the ways in which IDE II faced up to these difficulties. Details will be dealt with in subsequent chapters.

Instrumentation

Although the main set of instruments of IDE I and II is identical, in some cases we were forced to develop indices on the basis of slightly different or additional data. This was the case in order to tap labour market changes and technological developments on the organizational level and in order to measure respective factors on the macro-level.

Statistical Regression

Some indices in IDE II are somewhat less stable than in IDE I due to difficulties of obtaining requisite data. We will discuss this problem in due course.

Mortality

We had drop-outs on several levels. Only 10 of the original 12 countries participated in IDE II (missing: France and Italy, partly because of lacking research funding). Finland and Sweden had already conducted a replication in 1981. Yet another fully-fledged effort seemed impossible. Hence, for part of the Swedish companies we had to use their 1981 data as best estimates of the situation in the mid-80s despite the fact that their replication in 1981 did not yet contain the full set of new indices of IDE II. Some companies had gone bankrupt during the intermittent period; others were bought up by competitors. Some country teams of IDE I had also dissolved, so that new teams had to be developed and integrated into the international IDE Group.

Changing Population

It seems safe to assume that the universe of enterprises in the countries under study has, between the mid-seventies and mid-eighties, undergone a certain degree of change. However, neither is it easy to ascertain the specific nature and magnitude of that change, nor is it simple to speculate about the impact of global change upon the particular selection of enterprises in our study.

Measurement Points

To think of yet a third replication in the future is difficult to imagine given the average age of the IDE team-members, quite apart from the prohibitive cost factor.

Practical Problems

A few of the main problems were as follows. IDE was originally conceived as a synchronic study which turned into a diachronic research by default. Therefore, the data documentation of IDE I was insufficient for the needs of a later replication. Attempts to go back to IDE I to identify comparable data sets were often tantamount to archaeological chores.

Participating national teams in IDE II differed in points in time when funding became available. Obtaining international overhead support proved more cumbersome than anticipated. Both undermined the original time-schedule. Recent developments in data processing lead to slight differences in results such as in the case of treating missing values. In order to ensure standard procedures and to avoid processing errors IDE I data had to be recalculated with these more recent techniques. Floppy disks had become the preferred data carrier across national boundaries but we found that they got more easily lost or destroyed in the mail than the formerly used data tapes.

When it became known that the IDE International Research Group had embarked on a replication, colleagues in several other countries offered to co-operate in full realization that for them it would be an 'IDE I'. Although seven new country teams were interested to participate in the venture, in the end only sub-studies in Japan and Poland could be realized for some reason or other. However, at the least the studies in Poland and Japan constitute new cross-sectional studies from which certain, admittedly limited, conclusions can be drawn.

DATABASE

Size and industrial sector served as criteria to stratify the sample of establishments in IDE I. Size categories were small (100 permanent employees), middle (100–500), large (500–1,500). The 134 original establishments belonged either to the service (banking/insurance) or the metal engineering sector. Data collection of the original IDE I study took place 1975–7. The field-work of the replication (IDE II) was carried on between 1986 and 1987 in altogether 72 of the original 134 establishments. This set of 72 firms is fully comparable from IDE I to IDE II. In addition, 14 Swedish and 10 Finnish companies were restudied in 1981/2. For certain types of analysis these 24 firms can be added to the 72 fully matching ones, thus bringing the total to 96 organizations. The two 'new' IDE country teams from Japan and Poland respectively added 7 and 8 additional companies. Figure 1.5 illustrates the overall database for the results that will be reported in the following chapters.

The IDE International Research Group looks back at twenty years of co-operative efforts. Such a co-operation, which comprises a growing number of now close to thirty social scientists from some twenty research institutions of fourteen countries, is in itself rather unique. The functioning of this international research network became possible on

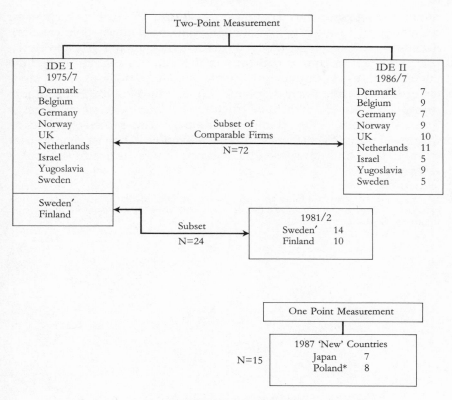

Fig. 1.5 Data Sets in IDE Research
* Four metal industry firms; the others are mineral, furniture, and chemical firms.

the basis of mutual trust which grew out of a collective understanding spelled out in a research organizational innovation—the 'social contract' (see IDE 1981*a*). A certain test of vitality of this co-operation is evident in the productivity of the team and its members in publishing research reports based on or related to joint efforts. A List of IDE publications is printed at the end of the present volume. However, much more crucial was the test to carry out IDE II. It is true, the IDE II study is but a partial replication of IDE I on less solid grounds. However, with the possibility of relating IDE I and IDE II the research became longitudinal—a feature often demanded and seldom fulfilled in social sciences. We found certain results in IDE II that further corroborate the findings of IDE I; but sometimes we did not, and as a consequence we had to modify our stance taken in IDE I. These are results, too. We felt them worth while to share with our readers. This is offered in the chapters to follow.

Chapter 2 will set the scene in terms of trying to reflect on the changes in the different national contexts of the IDE countries, changes that might impact upon participation in organizations: economic changes, technological advancement, industrial relations changes, political climate, and value changes. Chapter 3 presents the data of IDE I and II in a comparative, descriptive perspective; it illustrates changes over time and differences over countries.[2] Chapter 4 attempts to test various models of the dynamic interaction among the main variable in the study: Macro-variables, Participative Structure, Influence, and Contingencies. Thus, it attempts to shed some light into the intricate interactions of the factors relevant for participation in organizations. The last chapter tries to summarize and draw scientific and policy conclusions from the IDE research.

[2] When referring to results from participating establishments in the 1977 and 1987 empirical studies we will often use the term 'country' as a short version for 'companies in our study of country $X, Y, Z \ldots$'.

2

IDE Countries in Perspective

INTRODUCTION

The major aim of the 'Country context' chapter is to provide contextual background information and analysis related to the countries included in our study. This information is provided for the decade between the two waves of empirical IDE research: 1975/7–1986/7. The purpose of this information is to assist the readers of this book in the interpretation of the findings to be presented in the following chapters.

Since the *European Industrial Relations* (IDE 1981*b*) volume of the original study appeared, several important changes have taken place in the country context of industrial democracy. Some general European trends could also be detected. We hope to sketch out here the broad lines of development, to give illustrative examples of significant shifts where appropriate, and to highlight the key changes which have taken place during the decade of IDE research in the following areas; which, for the present study, represent the country contexts:

   (i) the political and economic background;
  (ii) the industrial relations system;
 (iii) the legislation in the field of industrial democracy; and finally
 (iv) the prevailing attitudes on participation.

The discussion by country in this chapter relates to the decade between the studies IDE I and IDE II. In principle, we limit our discussions to that period since the function of this chapter, according to the conceptual framework that guided our study, is to provide at least potential explanation and interpretation of the empirical findings which have emerged from the data that were collected in 1977/87. We are aware of course that remarkable developments took place in some IDE countries after 1987—for example, the severe economic and political crisis in Yugoslavia at the end of the 1980s, or the dramatic changes in West Germany before, during, and after the unification of the two Germanies. At the same time, dramatic developments occurred in other IDE countries. In those cases where post-1987 developments were perceived as having a strong influence on participatory systems in certain countries, some references are made to these developments in the following pages with the intention of completing and updating the picture.

It is difficult, if not impossible, to examine in one chapter all the developments that occurred during a decade in twelve countries and which, potentially at least, could have had an impact on the functioning of the existing Participative Structures (PS) and on their outcomes. Thus, instead of trying to include all contextual developments which took place in the IDE countries in the four areas mentioned above, we have attempted to present relevant examples of such contextual changes.

The brief model built into the 1981 publications, namely that 'the relevant background factors which influence and constitute the Industrial Relations System (IRS) in each country of which the Participative Structure PS is a reflection or consequence' (IDE 1981*a*: 3) must be discussed and it is still a useful one. Context can still be held to determine structure and 'is a necessary condition for the PS to function' (ibid.). Thus, we must examine what has been the change in the factors affecting the IRS and in turn the interrelations with changes in PS and attitudes to participation.[1]

AREAS OF CHANGE

In this section we present an overview of the major developments which took place during the 1977–87 decade. We hope that these country contexts can assist us in explaining and interpreting the findings of the parallel empirical studies conducted in the IDE countries.

The Political and Economic Background

The 1977–87 decade has seen a shift to the political Right in many IDE countries, as elsewhere in advanced economies, with some important exceptions, as we shall observe. This phenomenon of political conservatism may seem contradictory in light of the recession, but it is a fact. Its impact has been accompanied by a less hospitable attitude to trade unions and legislation designed to protect workers' rights and autonomy. There is, however, evidence of a 'ratchet effect' supporting existing participative structures (see Long & Warner 1987).

Several structural changes of an economic and commercial nature can be discerned during the period of study: increased international competition, increased role of multinational firms, shortening of product life-cycles, greater differentiation within product markets, increased importance of product quality and innovation, increase in the importance of the service sector *vis-à-vis* the manufacturing sector in the national

---

[1] An advanced draft of this chapter was distributed among the IDE research teams in the twelve countries. Their comments were incorporated into the final version presented in this book.

economy, the changing demographics of the work-force—especially the growing percentage of women (see Rojot 1989). These changes which characterized the 1977–87 decade have become even more visible in the very late 1980s.

During the last fifteen years or so, no country has been immune from the effects of the recession, although it has had differential impacts over recent years. Primarily, the rise in unemployment has chiefly affected the labour-markets of the countries involved. This change has had discernible affects on the strength of organized labour to bargain and has indeed diluted the level of unionization in most countries. In most of the countries which were included in our study, there have been chronic, relatively high rates of unemployment, pressures for greater labour productivity, a drop or stabilization in labour costs, a call for flexibility in wages, working hours, working conditions, and a restructuring of poorly competitive industries (for a more detailed analysis see Rojot 1989).

Unemployment rates are presented in Figure 2.1. It can be seen from the graph that during the 1978–87 decade there has been a more or less consistent increase in the rate of unemployment in all IDE countries (Poland not included in the table). The increase reached its peak in most countries in the years 1984–5. Countries with low unemployment rates during the 1978–87 period were: Sweden, Norway, and Japan; with medium rates: Israel, Finland, Federal Republic of Germany, and Denmark; with high rates: Yugoslavia, the Netherlands, Belgium, and the United Kingdom. The IDE country with the lowest unemployment rate was Norway (annual average of 2.3 per cent) and the country with the highest rate was Yugoslavia (12.8 per cent).

A comparison of unemployment in the IDE countries between the 1968–77 and the 1978–87 decades (see also Table 2.1) indicates an increase of unemployment in all IDE countries. There were, however, important differences among countries. In the Netherlands, United Kingdom, Belgium, and West Germany the ten-year (1978–87) percentage of unemployment had more than doubled, when compared to the previous decade. In Denmark, Yugoslavia, Finland, Israel, and Japan the increase was considerable, whereas in Norway and Sweden it was minor.

For more than the ten years under discussion, growth rates for OECD countries as a whole have decreased from an average of 4.5 per cent to between 2.5 and 3 per cent. Most experts expect (as suggested by Tavitian 1985) medium-term average rates of the order of 1.6–2 per cent for Western Europe (and around 3–3.5 per cent for the USA and Japan). 'For Western Europe at least, full employment is no longer an achievable target, social protection systems have to be substantially overhauled, and the traditional yearly increase in real wages has to be foregone for some time' (Tavitian 1985: 223).

IDE Countries in Perspective

TABLE 2.1. *General Level of Unemployment in the IDE Countries, excluding Poland, in the Years 1968–1987 (percentages)*

Country	Year 68	69	70	71	72	73	74	75	76	77	Average	Difference between Decades
Belgium	4.5	3.6	2.9	2.9	3.4	3.6	4.0	6.7	8.5	9.8	5.0	
Denmark						1.1	2.5	6.0	6.1	7.7	4.7	
Finland	4.0	2.8	1.9	2.3	2.5	2.3	1.7	2.2	4.0	6.1	3.0	
W. Germany	1.5	0.9	0.7	0.8	1.9	1.2	2.6	4.7	4.6	4.5	2.3	
Israel	6.1	4.5	3.8	3.5	2.7	2.6	3.0	3.1	3.6	3.9	3.7	
Japan	1.2	1.1	1.2	1.2	1.4	1.3	1.4	1.9	2.0	2.0	1.5	
Netherlands	1.9	1.4	1.1	1.6	2.7	2.7	3.6	5.2	5.5	5.3	3.1	
Norway					1.7	1.5	1.5	2.3	1.8	1.5	2.1	
Sweden	2.2	1.9	1.5	2.5	2.7	2.5	2.0	1.6	1.6	1.8	2.0	
UK	2.5	2.4	2.6	3.5	3.8	2.7	2.6	4.2	5.7	6.2	3.6	
Yugoslavia	8.0	8.2	7.7	6.7	7.0	8.1	9.0	10.2	11.4	11.9	8.8	

Country	78	79	80	81	82	83	84	85	86	87	Average	Difference between Decades
Belgium	7.9	8.2	8.9	10.9	12.7	14.0	14.1	13.3	12.3	11.9	11.4	6.4
Denmark	7.3	6.1	7.0	9.2	10.0	10.5	10.1	9.1	8.1	8.0	8.5	3.9
Finland	7.3	6.0	4.7	4.9	5.4	5.5	5.2	5.0	5.4	5.1	5.5	2.5
W. Germany	3.9	3.6	3.1	4.2	6.2	8.2	8.7	9.2	8.8		6.2	3.9
Israel	3.6	2.9	4.8	5.1	5.0	4.5	5.9	6.7	7.1	6.1	5.2	1.5
Japan	2.2	2.1	2.0	2.2	2.4	2.6	2.7	2.6	2.8	2.8	2.4	1.0
Netherlands	5.1	5.1	4.6	7.0	9.7	13.9	14.1	12.9	12.0	11.5	9.6	6.5
Norway	1.7	2.0	1.7	2.0	2.6	3.4	3.2	2.6	2.0	2.1	2.3	0.3
Sweden	2.3	2.1	2.0	2.5	3.2	3.5	3.1	2.8	2.2	1.9	2.6	0.5
UK	5.7	5.3	6.8	10.4	10.9	11.6	11.7	11.9	11.9		9.6	6.0
Yugoslavia	12.0	11.9	11.9	11.9	12.4	12.8	13.3	13.8	14.1	13.6	12.8	3.9

Source: Adapted from: ILO, *Year Book of Labour Statistics*, 38 (Geneva, 1978), table 9, for 1968–1977, and ibid. 48 (1988), table 9A for 1978–87. The unemployed comprise all persons above a specified age who during the reference period were without work, currently available for work, and seeking work. For details concerning the operative definitions in the various countries see issue 38, pp. 259–60, 268–78, and issue 48, pp. 617, 623–40. The percentages in the table illustrate the severity of unemployment within the fields covered by the respective series. They are calculated by relating the number of workers in the given group who are unemployed during the reference period (usually a particular day or a given week) to the total of employed and unemployed persons in the group at the same time.

In the first decade (1968–77) various sources were used. Source I: Labour-force sample surveys used in the case of Finland, Israel, Japan, Norway, Sweden. Source II: employment office statistics were used for Belgium, Denmark, W. Germany, Netherlands, UK, Yugoslavia.

In the second decade (1978–87). Source I: Labour-force sample surveys and general household sample surveys in the case of Finland, W. Germany, Israel, Japan, Norway, Sweden. Source II. Social insurance statistics in the case of UK. Source III1. Employment office statistics for Belgium, Denmark, Netherlands. Source III2. Employment office statistics in the case of Yugoslavia.

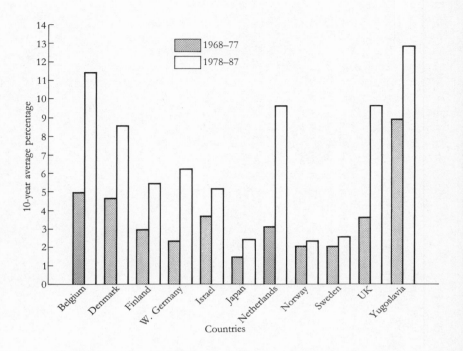

Fig. 2.1 General Level of Unemployment in IDE Countries, 1968–1987
Source: Adapted from ILO, *Year Book of Labour Statistics*, 38 (Geneva, 1978), table 9, for
1968–1977, and ibid. 48 (1988), table 9A for 1978–87. The unemployed comprise all persons
above a specified age who during the reference period were without work, currently
available for work, and seeking work. For details concerning the operative definitions in
the various countries see issue 38, pp. 259–260, 268–278, and issue 48, pp. 617, 623–40. The
percentages in the graph illustrate the severity of unemployment within the fields covered
by the respective series. They are calculated by relating the number of workers in the
given group who are unemployed during the reference period (usually a particular day
or a given week) to the total of employed and unemployed persons in the group at the
same time.
  In the first decade (1968–77) various sources were used. Source I: Labour-force sample
surveys used in the case of Finland, Israel, Japan, Norway, Sweden. Source II: employment
office statistics were used for Belgium, Denmark, W. Germany, Netherlands, UK, Yugoslavia. In the second decade (1978–87). Source I. Labour-force sample surveys and general
household sample surveys in the case of Finland, W. Germany, Israel, Japan, Norway,
Sweden. Source II. Social insurance statistics in the case of UK. Source III1. Employment
office statistics for Belgium, Denmark, Netherlands. Source III2. Employment office statistics in the case of Yugoslavia.

The involvement of workers in strikes and lock-outs in the IDE countries during the 1978–87 period is presented in Figure 2.2. The ratios
(workers involved divided by employment and multiplied by 100) indicate in 1978–87 a considerable variety by country. Annual average percentages enable us to divide the ten IDE countries into three major

groups: (*a*) Israel and Finland were characterized by high annual averages; (*b*) Denmark, the United Kingdom, Belgium, Sweden, and Norway were countries with medium averages; and (*c*) Japan, the Netherlands, and the Federal Republic of Germany stood out as countries with low average ratios.

A comparison of workers' involvement in strikes and lockouts between the two decades (see also Table 2.2) does not seem to reveal a consistent picture among the IDE countries. In six countries (Belgium, Denmark, West Germany, Israel, Norway, and Sweden) there has been an increase in workers' involvement in strikes and lockouts, but the rate of this increase varied considerably. Israel stands out both as a country with a very high involvement of workers in strikes during the 1978–87 decade and one in which that involvement increased very considerably (almost three times) when compared to the previous decade. On the

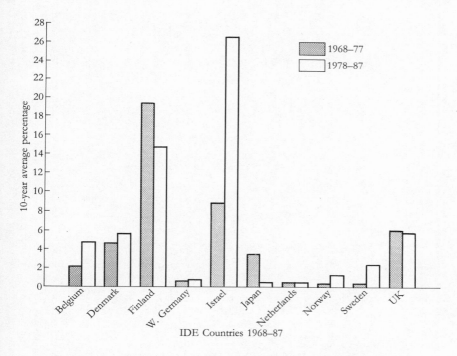

Fig. 2.2 Workers' Involvement in Strikes and Lock-outs, 1968–1987
Source: Adapted from: ILO, *Year Book of Labour Statistics*, 38 (Geneva, 1978), tables 4 and 24, for 1968–1977 and ibid. 48. (1988), tables 3 and 30, for 1978–87. The involvement of workers in strikes and lock-outs was computed by dividing the number of workers involved in strikes and lock-outs in a certain year by the total number of civilian persons employed in the same year. The statistics are of various types and in general a certain element of estimation is involved in their compilation (for a more detailed information see ILO, *Year Book of Labour Statistics*, 48 (Geneva, 1988), p. 200.

TABLE 2.2. Workers' Involvement in Strikes and Lock-outs in IDE Countries, excluding Poland and Yugoslavia, in the Years 1966–1987 (percentages)

Country	68	69	70	71	72	73	74	75	76	77	Average
Belgium	0.00	0.00	2.94	2.35	1.80	1.66	1.47	2.29	2.87	1.77	2.14
Denmark	0.00	0.00	0.00	0.00	0.32	14.13	6.05	2.54	3.65	1.50	4.70
Finland	0.00	0.00	9.48	19.00	11.32	31.34	16.63	9.69	22.97	34.99	19.43
Germany	0.10	0.35	0.70	2.05	0.09	0.71	0.97	0.14	0.69	0.14	0.59
Israel	4.63	4.70	11.93	8.85	8.34	11.18	2.48	10.26	10.20	16.76	8.93
Japan	2.33	2.80	3.38	3.70	3.01	4.25	6.91	5.23	2.57	1.30	3.55
Netherlands	0.00	0.28	1.15	0.78	0.43	1.28	0.07	0.01	0.34	0.79	0.51
Norway	0.04	0.07	0.26	0.00	0.07	0.14	1.34	0.19	1.21	0.13	0.38
Sweden	0.01	0.24	0.69	1.63	0.19	0.11	0.44	0.58	0.21	0.32	0.44
UK	9.24	6.80	7.39	4.90	7.22	6.21	6.58	3.29	2.73	0.00	6.04

Country	78	79	80	81	82	83	84	85	86	87	Average	Difference between Decades
Belgium	5.20	5.66	3.48	0.00	0.00	0.00	0.00	0.00	0.00	0.00	4.78	2.63
Denmark	2.40	6.42	0.00	2.26	0.00	1.71	2.04	22.77	2.13	0.00	5.68	0.98
Finland	7.23	9.84	17.26	20.50	6.89	17.36	22.88	6.89	23.96	0.00	14.76	−4.67
Germany	1.87	0.29	0.17	0.94	0.15	0.36	2.02	0.29	0.43	0.00	0.72	0.13
Israel	18.50	20.18	7.29	24.63	64.60	14.06	38.90	35.13	15.74	0.00	26.56	17.63
Japan	1.22	0.82	1.02	0.44	0.38	0.39	0.27	0.21	0.20	0.17	0.51	−3.04
Netherlands	0.21	0.77	0.52	0.17	1.39	0.41	0.32	0.44	0.33	0.24	0.48	−0.03
Norway	0.24	0.15	0.98	0.22	1.27	0.06	1.56	0.33	7.95	0.12	1.29	0.90
Sweden	0.20	0.77	17.64	2.35	0.12	0.34	0.56	0.29	1.54	0.24	2.41	1.96
UK	4.16	18.15	3.29	6.21	8.80	2.28	6.09	3.24	2.94	3.55	5.87	−0.17

The involvement of workers in strikes and lock-outs was computed by dividing the number of workers involved in strikes and lock-outs in a certain year by the total number of civilian persons employed in the same year. The statistics are of various types and in general a certain element of estimation is involved in their compilation (for a more detailed information see ILO, Year Book of Labour Statistics, 48 (Geneva, 1988), 200.

other hand, in West Germany the involvement of workers in strikes and lockouts during the 1978–87 decade was low and its increase, compared to the previous decade, was very minor (0.13 per cent). In three countries (Finland, Japan, and the United Kingdom) there has been during the 1980s a decrease in the involvement of workers in strikes and lockouts, and in the Netherlands there has practically been no change. Although the picture concerning the involvement in strikes and lockouts does not reflect a clear pattern the situation in the individual countries may be an important contextual factor contributing to the interpretation of our findings in this study.

The average annual change over previous years of Gross Domestic Product (GDP) (in percentages), as an indicator of economic growth, is presented in Figure 2.3 (see also Table 2.3). It can be seen from the Figure 2.3 that in the 1978–87 decade there were relatively high average annual increases of GDP in Japan, Norway, and Finland; medium increases in Sweden, United Kingdom, Denmark, and West Germany; and relatively

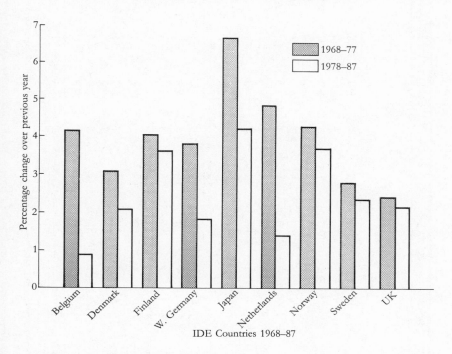

Fig. 2.3 Gross Domestic Product in Constant Prices for IDE Countries, excluding Israel, Poland, and Yugoslavia, 1968–1987

Source: Adapted from: IMF, *International Financial Statistics Yearbook 1990* (Washington, DC, Aug. 1990), 162–65. Data concerning Poland and Yugoslavia are not available and data concerning Israel are incomplete. GNP is used in calculation for Japan. Constant prices are calculated as percentage change over previous year calculated from indexes.

TABLE 2.3. *Gross Domestic Product in Constant Prices for IDE Countries, excluding Israel, Poland, and Yugoslavia, 1968–1987*

Country	Year										Average	Difference between Decades
	68	69	70	71	72	73	74	75	76	77		
Belgium	4.3	6.6	6.3	3.7	5.4	5.9	4.3	-1.5	5.7	0.6	4.13	
Denmark	3.8	6.5	2.3	2.4	5.4	3.8	-0.9	-0.7	6.5	1.6	3.07	
Finland	2.3	9.6	7.5	2.1	7.6	6.7	3.0	1.1	0.3	0.1	4.03	
W. Germany	6.3	7.5	5.1	2.9	4.2	4.7	0.3	-1.6	5.4	3.0	3.78	
Japan	12.5	12.1	9.5	4.3	8.5	7.9	-1.4	2.7	4.8	5.3	6.62	
Netherlands	6.5	12.4	5.7	4.2	3.3	4.7	4.0	-0.1	5.1	2.3	4.81	
Norway	2.3	4.5	2.0	4.6	5.2	4.1	5.2	4.2	6.8	3.6	4.25	
Sweden	3.6	5.0	6.6	0.9	2.3	4.0	3.2	2.7	1.1	-1.6	2.78	
UK	4.2	1.3	2.8	2.8	2.4	7.7	-1.0	-0.7	3.7	1.0	2.42	
	78	79	80	81	82	83	84	85	86	87		
Belgium	2.9	2.2	4.1	-9.0	1.5	0.4	2.1	0.9	1.8	2.0	0.89	-3.24
Denmark	1.5	3.5	-0.4	-0.9	3.0	2.5	4.4	4.3	3.6	-0.6	2.09	-0.98
Finland	2.2	7.3	5.4	1.6	3.6	3.0	3.3	3.5	2.3	3.8	3.60	-0.43
West-Germany	2.9	4.1	1.4	0.2	-0.6	1.5	2.8	2.0	2.3	1.8	1.84	-1.94
Japan	5.2	5.3	4.3	3.7	3.1	3.2	5.1	4.7	2.7	4.6	4.19	-2.43
Netherlands	2.5	2.4	0.9	-0.7	-1.4	1.4	3.2	2.6	2.0	1.1	1.40	-3.41
Norway	4.5	5.1	4.2	0.9	0.3	4.6	5.7	5.3	4.2	1.8	3.66	-0.59
Sweden	1.8	3.8	1.7		1.1	1.8	4.0	2.2	2.2	2.6	2.36	-0.42
UK	3.9	2.3	-1.9	-1.1	1.3	3.7	1.8	3.8	3.5	4.4	2.17	-0.25

Source: Adapted from *International Financial Statistics Yearbook 1990*, (Washington, DC, Aug. 1990), 162–5.
Data concerning Poland and Yugoslavia are not available and the data concerning Israel are incomplete. GNP is used in calculation for Japan Constant Prices calculated as percentage change over previous year calculated from indexes.

low increases in Belgium and the Netherlands. When the average annual increases of GDP of 1968–77 are compared with those of the 1978–87 decade a consistent pattern emerges. In all IDE countries (Israel, Poland, and Yugoslavia are not included due to lack of suitable data) the percentage averages in the second decade (1978–87) were lower than those of the first (1968–77), i.e. economic growth, as measured by increase in GDP, was lower in the 1980s than in 1970s. The differences between the two decades (averages of the 1978–87 minus averages of the 1968–78 decade) in the IDE countries ranged between – 3.44 percent (in the Netherlands) and – 0.25 percent (in the United Kingdom), but the trend was consistent across countries.

In almost all the countries included in our study, political and economic conditions which existed during the period under discussion have often exerted pressures on the trade unions to restrain their demands. In general, the change towards more conservative governments and settings does not seem to encourage the flourishing of representative participation structures, whereas the impact of the economic structural changes may encourage such structures in some countries, industries, and organizations and impede their development in others.

The Industrial Relations Systems

In order to understand the background to the IDE data presented, we need to comment on the changes in the Industrial Relations Systems in the countries concerned. The interrelationships between the major actors on the industrial relations scene are an instrinsic part of the social system of each country. Still some cross-country generalization can be made. Albeda (1984), for example, after examining European industrial relations in a time of crisis (referring to the 1980s), concludes his review by suggesting three such major generalizations:

1. Governments have become more active in the field of collective bargaining and they have often tried to regulate its process.
2. There has been a change in the power relations: trade unions tend to be losing their power in the labour market as well as in the political field.
3. There has been a growing awareness of governments, employers, and unions that something should be done about the growth of unemployment and the rigidities of the labour market.

In a recent examination of the industrial relations systems of several OECD countries, a most interesting attempt was made to evaluate the extent to which the political-, economic-, and social-structured changes which occurred in these countries have reinforced or transformed their existing industrial relations systems (Rojot 1989). This evaluation suggests that the Federal Republic of Germany and Japan present the distinctive characteristics that the main features of their industrial relations systems have not been weakened by the structural changes, or have even been reinforced by the impact of these changes. On the other hand, in countries such as the United Kingdom and the Netherlands the industrial relations systems were not able to resist the structural changes which have taken place in recent years. In these cases the impact of change introduced meaningful transformations. In the less resistant systems, the actor who gave impetus to the structural changes varies according to the case. For example, in the United Kingdom the (Conservative) government has been the most involved actor in the transformation process and it did so in its dual role as legislator and employer. In the Netherlands, so it seems, the structural changes have affected the industrial relations systems through the combined efforts of a weakened trade union movement with a centre-Right government.

It should be kept in mind, however, that the typological distinction between the two kinds of reactions of the industrial relations system to structural changes is probably more a matter of degree than of nature. Other conclusions drawn from this analysis are as follows.

1. There is an increasing internal segmentation of industrial relations systems in the various countries, and internal variance of industrial relations in a specific country is growing, mainly on the basis of economic sections.
2. There is a tendency to decentralize industrial relations towards the enterprise level.
3. As far as the rate of unionization is concerned, the situation varies. It is stable or has even increased somewhat in the Federal Republic of Germany of the years before unification, but has declined, for example, in the Netherlands, Japan, and the United Kingdom.

In many countries, the policies of the employers have become dominant. The employer is also the component in the industrial relations systems who can, more than before the mid-seventies 'choose to try operating with or without a union, to integrate the policy of personnel and strategy, and to continue to operate within a model of co-determination or not to . . . he seems to have become the dominant actor in industrial relations in the majority of cases' (Rojot 1989: 14). Still, in spite of the fact that most of the initiatives to introduce flexibility in the employment of workers in industry and services have come from the employers, the flexibility issue constitutes an important challenge to unions. The development of economic and social programmes that look to the future fall especially on the shoulders of the central trade union organizations, who are expected to design innovative labour strategies in the field of employment (see also Kassalow 1987).

National Legislation in the Field of Industrial Democracy

The main changes affecting PS over the period 1976–86 vary from country to country. A claim can be made that in principle where PS are largely underpinned by statutory safeguards, the potential for participation has been less undermined than where *de facto* involvement in decision-making depends only on labour-market strength. Still the question remains: should a country legislate to encourage industrial democracy, or is there a better way? Nowadays, as some writers who recently reviewed the international scene claim, the issue is not so clear and most countries seem to stick to their established practice, at least where major changes are involved (Monat and Sarfati 1986). Several industrialized countries, like France and the Netherlands, have between 1977 and 1987 adopted legislation on participation in the form of employees' right of expression. Also, under a 1982 Act in the United Kingdom, enterprises with more than 250 employees are required to submit an annual report on steps taken to introduce, maintain, or promote workers' participation, but this is basically only a formality. Of course, since the 1950s, the Federal Republic of Germany and Yugoslavia have had a long tradition of legislation in the field of industrial democracy. Moreover, in Sweden, which traditionally favoured national agreements, new rules for participation were laid down by a 1976 Act.

According to a 1983 study, the most significant potential impact of new technologies upon changes in industrial relations concerns the development of participation and joint control. It pushes trade unions towards the co-operative and legalistic approach (Commission of the European Communities 1983). Still, efforts to harmonize the national legislation of the members of the European Communities in the area of workers' participation have by now quite a long history (see Pipkon 1984). This was done largely through the draft 'Fifth Directive' on company law, but the harmonization efforts have not yet borne fruit.

The participation of workers' representatives on the board of directors and supervisory boards, has been established on the basis of legislation, collective agreement, or on employers' initiative. There have recently been claims that the trends of the 1960s and early 1970s seem to have reversed somewhat nowadays, when less importance is apparently attached to workers' representation at board level than in the past, at least in the private sector. Further, it is claimed that the most effective design for workers' representation at board level is not yet in place (Stem 1988; Monat and Sarfati 1986). On the other hand, workers' representation on the boards of public enterprises is still in vogue and takes place in industrialized as well as in developing countries. Evidence from various countries included in our study indicates that interesting learning processes, especially for employees but also for top managers, are a result of that participative mode.

Works Councils of various kinds seem very important in a large number of countries. A major reason for the interest in them is probably the need felt by the employers to involve the work-force in the crucial process of the introduction of new technologies, a process which is firmly related to the pressures of the international market. In some countries, work councils were backed by legislation, as for example in the Netherlands, where work councils have been extended to small enterprises, or in France (which is not included in the second phase of the IDE project), where work councils were set up for groups of enterprises. In other countries, as for example in Denmark, the role of work councils has been strengthened, not through laws but rather through collective agreements. Also in the United Kingdom in recent years joint consultative bodies have made a strong comeback in some private sector companies. There the initiative was often taken by the employers. In several countries, judgements have been handed down by courts that define more clearly the powers of work councils. The Federal Republic of Germany is a good example here.

In the country reports, we shall examine changes which took place in the major bases of participative structures during the decade 1976–1986. Major emphasis will be put on legislation activity, but we shall naturally include in our country-by-country examination the role played by collective agreements in the development of participation. We shall relate in the country examination to both the national and enterprise levels.

Prevailing Attitudes towards Participation

The 'Green Book' published by the Commission of the European Communities relates, among other things, to the ethical approach to workers' participation by suggesting that

Decisions taken by or in the enterprise can have a substantial effect on their economic circumstances both immediately and in the long term; the satisfaction which they [their employees] derive from work, their health and physical condition; the time and energy which they can devote to their families and to activities other than work; and even their sense of dignity and autonomy as human beings. Accordingly continuing consideration is being given to the problem of how and to what extent employees should be able to influence decisions of enterprises which employ them. (Bulletin of the European Communities 1975: 8)

According to this argument, workers have the right to be heard on matters connected with the operation of the enterprise in view of the facts that they play an important part in production and that their entire life is influenced by their work sale.

But the present interest in methods of participation in Western societies exists not only because of ethical considerations. Practical approaches are not less important. For example, it has become more and more recognized during recent decades that due to the increased standard of education and normative changes the younger generation who are entering the labour-force are increasingly unwilling to accept authority and decisions over which they have no influence. A higher skill-profile in enterprises, especially the high-tech ones, will increase the *de facto* power of employees *vis-à-vis* day to day operations (see Warner 1989). Being on the receiving end at work is not considered to be a desirable status for the more educated personnel. The negative motivational implications of a non-participative managerial approach are of concern not only to subordinates but also to management itself. Also, as mentioned earlier in this chapter, the introduction of new technologies—which is so vital for market competitiveness—can be highly facilitated by employing participative methods of various types. In this connection one of the major conclusions of a comparative survey which was conducted in Europe in the 1980s by the *European Foundation for the Improvement of Living and Working Conditions* is that there are clear indications that social dialogue in Europe, in relation to technological change, is already an extended practice. The attitudes of managements and workers' representatives are in general positive 'both in terms of their appreciation of the past experience and of their willingness to enter into further dialogue' (Di Martino 1987: 30). However, important differences do exist among the various countries. Although employers in European countries often continue to oppose formal joint-decision methods, as, for example, board representation of employees and joint management boards, they have developed, so it seems, more positive attitudes towards direct methods of participation which take place at the shop-floor level.

The Economic and Social Committee of the European Communities unanimously agreed in 1978 that employee participation in the broadest sense of the term is a desirable development in a democratic society (for a more detailed discussion see Hanami and Monat 1988). We believe implied in such a decision is that a democratic society by its very nature cannot accept a meaningful qualitative difference between the status of people as citizens and as employees. Thus, the right of the citizen to exert influence on the rulers should have some parallel right at the organizational setting of work. 'It is even not uncommon', conclude Hanami and Monat (1988: 13), 'that the issue of employee participation is stated in terms of distribution or redistribution of power in the enterprise as between the employees and the employer.' The extent to which the employees themselves and their representatives are aware of and reject the gap between their status as citizens and employees is not clear. It seems that the question has not been subjected to broad empirical study.

In the country reports, we shall try to analyse the main changes in prevailing attitudes towards participation. Our interest should be to learn about the attitudes not only of managers and workers and of their representatives, but also about the attitudes towards industrial demo- cracy which prevail among important components of the environment of work organizations such as the general public, influential political groups, trade unions, and employers' associations. However, it seems quite difficult to find empirical studies which examine systematically the attitudes of the parties involved. In most countries the discussion will focus on two levels: the macro level where various types of national agreements between the employers, the unions, and often the govern- ment take place, and the micro, i.e. company and plant, level. Generally speaking, it would seem that interest in industrial democracy has waned since the 1970s, although it has surfaced as an issue rather more in some countries than others, and even received new impetus in some countries.

On the management side, those managements and managers who feel concerned by employee participation have adopted one or more of the following justifications or reasons for their concern:

 (i) the need to improve by means of participative measures the com- petitiveness of their firms in the local or international markets;

 (ii) the necessity to adapt to the changes which have taken place among the present work-force that has become more educated and has developed new expectations; and

(iii) participation as a positive value in its own sake based on philo- sophical and ethical considerations (see Rojot 1987; Rosenstein 1989).

Still, it seems that in areas such as economic and financial policy of the firm and questions of general policy which have to do with the structure of the firm and its very existence, employers are strongly inclined to maintain decisions within the scope of management prerogatives, whereas in relation to personnel questions and various daily operational issues they may be more inclined to accept and even encourage various participative methods.

The attitude of trade unions towards industrial democracy, in the IDE study countries during the period under discussion in this volume, seemed to range between support and indifference. Their major efforts have been to preserve and sometimes even to strengthen the collective- bargaining process, but they have often been acting under the con- straints of difficult economic conditions and in several countries under pressures exerted by conservative governments. Shop-floor participa- tion methods, which actually constitute part of the 'Quality of Working Life' concept, have been met with suspicion by unions in some countries which saw in them a threat to their influence in the enterprise. A large number of European unions tended to consider that programme for improving the quality of life at work have at least mixed objectives (see Institut Syndical Européen 1980). Even when unions assume that certain shop-floor innovations can be beneficial to the employees, they may prefer bargaining on them and not allowing management unilateral decision-making.

COUNTRY REPORTS

In this section, country by country reports are presented. The discussion will focus on the developments which took place in the IDE countries within the four areas of change which were examined in the previous section. As mentioned earlier, post-1986 developments will be referred to only in some country reports.

Belgium

In Belgium, coalition governments prevailed and in the election of December 1987 there was a fall in the Christian Democratic vote and a rise in support for the Socialists. Decentralization led to the establishment of regional governments with national government governing with full powers, and governmental intervention in the social negotiations. The Belgian pluralistic trade union movement has grown up around two major confederations, the Socialist and the Christian, and a smaller one, the confederation of Liberal Trade Unions. The movement derives its strength from a high level of union membership (about 70 per cent of the labour-force) and from participation in national economic and social policy-making bodies (Gevers 1987).

There has been a tendency lately towards increasing involvement of the social partners—employers and trade unions—on their own initiative or on the government's initiative, in recovery issues such as work-time reduction, youth employment, and vocational training. But in 1980 Belgium imposed a wage freeze on the social partners for the first time. The government has encouraged private initiatives and avoided saving firms at risk by making them publicly owned. Flanders and Wallonia respectively have pursued different paths of economic development.

At the level of the enterprise, works councils and possible trade union delegations are to be informed before the introduction of new technologies, about the nature of the technology, the consequences concerning the number of jobs, the involved human relations, personnel policy transfers, and training. However, the employees have no right to negotiate on the introduction of new technologies (Blanpain 1983).

In Belgium, both social partners participate at the national level in the shaping of economic and social policies. The National Labour council is made up of an equal number of unions and employers' representatives and concludes nation-wide agreements involving diverse matters such as minimum wages, maximum number of hours per week, etc. Some of the most noteworthy agreements resulted in the works councils being given the right to extensive information. As a result of these and other agreements between the unions and employers, there have been relatively few conflicts in Belgium (Jain, *et al.*, 1980; Gevers 1987). Most collective bargaining is handled at a national, industrial, or sector-wide level. Union delegations operate at the shop-floor level and once they have been granted permission by the employer they can negotiate collective agreements which supplement national agreements. From 1976 the government started intervening in the collective-bargaining process. The period from 1973 to 1981 witnessed crisis, deadlocked collective bargaining, and the first intervention of the state. Observers believe that the deadlocks were due to several factors among which were the combination of unemployment (risen from 5 per cent 1973–7 to 13.4 per cent 1983–6) and recession, as well as a hardening of the differences between economically strong and economically weak sectors. Collective bargaining began to shift towards the regions and the shop-floor. With the inability of employers and unions to find a common ground, the state would relinquish its role of 'facilitator' and institute an incomes' policy. The Social–Christian–Liberal coalitions in 1981 and 1985 enabled the government to take more drastic measures than its predecessors in collective bargaining in terms of both the scope and the methods of action.

In fact, the government began to take a major role in collective bargaining (Beaupain 1987). Unions have put forward their request for an overall collective agreement covering all aspects and giving the employees more impact on the decision to introduce new technologies and on the consequences thereof (see Blanpain 1983).

The general decentralization of Belgium into regions and communities (Flanders, Wallonia, and Brussels) affects the industrial relations system. New regional bodies are established and the social partners become decentralized too. Sometimes, competition arises between social partners' associations on the national and regional levels.

During the decade under study there have been changes in legislation on participation, the most important of which deal with the functions and composition of the works council. The informative and consultative roles of the works councils have been extended. In addition, the works councils received a new role from the government, namely, controlling the effect of recovery measures at the firm level. Specific legislation (1985) changed the composition of works councils by giving managerial personnel the right to be represented in a works council as a separate delegation (independent from the employer). Belgian works councils will thus be composed of: representatives of the employer on the one side, and elected members for workers, white-collar employees, and managerial personnel on the other. The managerial personnel can present candidates for the social elections through managers' associations or on an individual basis: this means that for managerial personnel, union membership is not a condition for becoming a member of the works council.

An area in which workers' influence was promoted by legislation in Belgium is industrial medicine. Under 1979 legislation on industrial medicine, workers' representatives on safety committees and trade union officials can have a works' doctor replaced if he fails to perform his duties properly, or has lost the confidence of the workers.

In times of recovery measures (including the scaling down of wages and social security) Belgian unions seem to have had fights to win over other issues than participation, particularly in Belgium. On the shop-floor, movements such as employee involvement and quality circles create other (parallel and competitive) networks of workers.

Employers' associations are primarily concerned with regaining competitive power for firms and ensuring their survival, so that they prefer to remain quiet about participation. The government is pushing with full powers towards a recovery policy and is putting pressure on the social partners to reach agreements fitting into this policy: if agreements are not reached sufficiently quickly or effectively, the government makes the decisions itself.

At the overall societal level, democratization seemed to be decreasing. As examples we could note: the restricted power of parliament; scaling back of the social security system; and lower participation in education by lower socio-economic levels. Few agreements were reached at national level, unless under pressure from the government. Most collective-bargaining agreements were reached at branch level.

Denmark

In Denmark, a coalition (minority) government of Conservatives, Farmers, Centre-Democrats, and Christians took over without elections from a Social Democratic minority government in December 1982. This government was strengthened by the national election of 1984 and has stayed in power with the support of the Social Liberals. It gave priority to a balanced budget and a reduction in the rate of inflation, but it was less successful in reducing the deficit of the balance of payments. In consequence, the fear of increasing unemployment due to monetary policies was not warranted and the rate of unemployment decreased since a maximum in 1983.

No long-term left- or right-wing wave has been seen in the Danish Folketing/Parliament. During the period 1977–84, the Social Democrats have been weakened and the Socialist Peoples' Party strengthened. So all in all, these two parties, together with other small left-wing parties, had 47 per cent of the votes, both at the beginning and at the end of the period 1977–84. On the other hand, a movement away from the small parties on the left and right sides of the party system can be seen. This development is parallel to a decrease in distrust towards politicians and less political alienation compared to the beginning of the 1970s.

In the labour-market, one could note an increase in the female activity rate, especially among married women. In 1983, 67 per cent of married women were gainfully employed. At the same time, fewer men than in 1976 stayed in the labour-market. As about 40 per cent of the women were employed part-time, this change in the distribution of the labour-force may be expected to decrease the involvement of workers at the firm level.

On the other hand, the percentage of organized workers and white-collar employees has not been reduced as might be expected, due to the changed composition of the labour-force and as a consequence of high unemployment. On the contrary, the percentage of organized wage earners increased from 65 in 1976 to 84 in 1982, but the rate was clearly higher among those with more than a 30-hour week, namely, 89 in 1982. In 1986, around 90 to 95 per cent of the male workers and 75 per cent of female workers were organized (Hansen 1986: 57).

During the years 1976–86 industrial change (a relative growth of the services sector, the continuous implementation of information techno-logy, and high unemployment) has posed a new challenge to relations between employers and employees at all levels. In particular these changes raised the question of the tendency towards a demand for a higher degree of labour flexibility.

At the national level, the government has intervened four times in the biennial negotiations about collective agreements (in 1977, 1979, and 1985). The state's intervention did bring a decrease in real wages. 'Tri-partite bodies were inherent in many institutions created to implement an active labour market policy based on the Swedish model as a supple-ment to general economic policies' (Lind 1988: 6).

Inability to reduce unemployment was softened by a relatively high level of unemployment benefit compared to wages. This change together with various programmes to some extent ensured that unem-ployment did not result in serious social disaster (see Lind 1988).

Open conflicts were still an important part of the industrial relations picture in Denmark even though the level of unofficial strikes was lower during the 1980s than in the 1970s. In 1985, a major conflict between the Danish Federation of Trade Unions (LO) and the Danish Employers' Confederation (DA) members took place following a breakdown of the negotiations about the renewal of collective agreements. As a con-sequence of this impasse, the government, supported by the bourgeois majority, enacted new terms for the labour market, but under protest from LO and after a series of unofficial strikes. Since 1976, the government has legislated on wage rates, etc. three times (in 1977, 1979, and 1985) whereas the labour market organizations, with the help of the State Mediator, renewed the collective agreements in 1981, 1983, and 1987. Workers' real wages and disposable income have fallen during the decade 1977–86 and in general the trade union movement has had difficulties in making any strong initiatives during the last decade. Its much-debated proposal on economic democracy and a wage earners' collective fund has lately been turned into profit-sharing on an individual basis by some major firms, and a government proposal along these lines is expected.

The inability to reduce unemployment, which rose especially from 1981, was softened in Denmark by a relatively high level of unemployment benefit compared to wages and by programmes to employ the most vulnerable groups among the unemployed youth and long-term unemployed, mainly women and unskilled workers (Lind 1988). Unemployment benefits were most severely cut under the conservative–liberal government which took office in 1982. In the 1980s the employers fulfilled their long-time wish for removal of the automatic cost of living adjustment, and collective bargaining was decentralized when several times negotiations were left in the hands of individual national trade unions and DA's member organizations. The trade union movement as a whole has none the less not lost its influence as an important base of power. Membership figures have been increasing until 1987. It is estimated that agreements at industry level may also in the future be accepted broadly in the trade union movement but that no further decentralization will take place (Lind 1988).

The Company Act of 1973 which gave two employees representation at company board level in Denmark was changed in 1980, so employees now have one-third of the membership at board level in companies with more than fifty employees. In 1981, the Agreement between the Danish Federation of Trade Unions and the Danish Employers' Confederation on Co-operation and Co-operation Committees of 1970 was supplemented by an agreement on technology. The new agreement stressed the responsibilities of management regarding information on new technology and technological changes to be given in advance of implemented changes. In the event of loss of jobs, the firm must try to replace the workers within the firm. The firm will have to help workers with retraining opportunities in cases of dismissals. Organizations outside LO and DA negotiated similar or better agreements, seen from the employers' point of view.

In 1986, both LO and DA negotiated a new agreement (the earlier one was signed in 1981) on co-operation including technology. One major change was the possibility of firms with thirty-five or more employees to establish co-operation committees if one of the parties wanted them. Previously the limit was fifty employees. Another change was an extension of information from management to workers and the responsibility of the representatives of the workers to inform the co-operation committee about work-place conditions.

According to the Danish survey, more workers in 1983 than in 1976 felt that they had no influence upon such matters as fixing breaks, rationalizations, acquisitions of major equipment, job appointments and dismissals, promotions, premises and hygiene, and future production and employment at the place of work. In most instances, 70–90 per cent of the workers had no influence on the above-mentioned matters in 1983. On the other hand, the workers perceived more influence upon the arrangement of daily work in 1983 than in 1976. Survey results confirm this development with regard to skilled workers and employees also for 1986, but the difference in influence for unskilled workers in 1986 compared with 1976 is small, as the result of a widening difference in influence between high status and low status employees (Hansen 1986).

To some extent these changes may be due to increased expectations regarding influence and the understanding of its meaning. On the other hand, we have some evidence of a change in management style during the late 1970s and early 1980s *inter alia* exemplified by the drop in the number of joint consultation committees during the period 1978–82, when the economic crisis was deeply felt.

New technology and its social consequences, as well as work environment questions in general, had become important issues in the labour-market during the decade under study. This change is due to the implementation of the work environment legislation of 1975, and a general awareness of serious work hazards caused, for examples by new chemical substances. Survey results show that the work environment in general has neither improved nor deteriorated from 1976 to 1986 (ibid.).

Federal Republic of Germany

The decade between 1977 and 1987 in the Federal Republic of Germany saw an important political change following the 1982 Federal elections: a switch from a Social (Democratic)–Liberal to a Conservative (Christian-Democratic)–Liberal government with the emergence of a new iconoclastic political group, Environmentalists, being represented in the Federal Parliament. Government supply-oriented economic and financial policy led to growth and more employment. Two typical measures were: first, the reduction of labour market obstacles which are considered to hinder employment, like allowing temporary appointments and part-time working, the idea being that existing laws in the area of work impede liberalization of enterprise employment policies. And secondly, instead of a programme to support employment, the present Liberal–Conservative government believed in the effectiveness of tax reforms which lead to more investment on the company side. One aim was thus to create more jobs. Complementary tax reform measures were assumed to take effect only later.

On the economic front, during the period in question, a doubling of unemployment rates has occurred (from 4.6 per cent in 1976 to 9.2 per cent in 1985). While for the first time the gross national product has developed independently from unemployment rates, first falling with increased unemployment then growing at the rate of 2 per cent and more.

At the company level, the 1976–86 decade brought both unprecedented frequencies of bankruptcies and an unprecedented national and international merger of German companies. The ratio of foreign workers in the German work force between 1976 and 1986 dropped by 20 per cent to an overall 7.5 per cent (Bundesanstalt für Arbeit 1987). There are now about twice the number of foreign workers who leave the FRG as arrive (but most recently there has been an influx of East Germans and ethnic Germans from the Ukraine.)

Manufacturing industries still play a very important role in West Germany, although in the period from 1974 to 1987 1.4 million jobs were lost in the manufacturing industries and the service sector increased the volume of its jobs by 1.6 million. In 1987, 21.045 million people were employed (excluding civil servants), and among those nearly 48 per cent were still employed in manufacturing industries. White-collar workers increased from 41.8 per cent in 1980 to 44 per cent in 1987. This change 'seems to be slower and less dramatic than in many other countries' (Weiss 1989). Full-time employment for an indefinite period was still the normal case in West Germany. The only attempt at deregulation in this area is the Act on Improvement of Employment Opportunities of May 1985. It has facilitated fixed contracts and temporary work and has encouraged part-time employment, but they still remained marginal.

The so-called concerted action, a tripartite arrangement (more or less informal meetings of top representatives of the federal state, the trade unions, and the employers' associations) was abolished in the late 1970s. However, the corporatist framework was re-established by means of regular but separate meetings between the employers and government, as well as between the trade unions and the government (Weiss 1989).

At the level of the industrial relations systems, the West German Co-Determination Act of 1976 (affecting only large companies with more than 2,000 employees) has led to a breakdown of the formerly existing 'concerted action' of co-operation among social partners on the national level. The state of stalemate continued throughout the decade under

study. Discoveries of economic mismanagement in union-owned housing construction companies led to a decrease of public trust in unions
and a commensurate loss of prestige. The introduction of new technologies has contributed to decentralization—a shift of the negotiation
level from regional/national levels to within-company bargaining. As a
consequence, official union policies are hard to maintain against local
pressures. The trend is further fostered by a new law forbidding unemployment pay for locked-out workers. The change in law was in 1985
and concerns workers whose enterprise stops producing because of
strikes in other firms, which lead to a shortage of raw materials. After
the reformation of the law, the union instead of the company must now
pay these workers. In West Germany, the government is not allowed to
intervene in pay negotiations between both sides of industry (the parties
even provide their own voluntary conciliations system). The unions look
upon this change as having a weakening effect on their possibilities and,
hence, as an offence against the spirit of industrial relations law.

In principle, trade union policy is 'co-operative' in so far as the unions
receive information and are consulted about all major areas of social and
economic policy. As a result, 'the West Germany unions are not only
powerful partners in collective bargaining, but they also exert great
influence on political and social life' (Fürstenberg 1987: 169).

In the 1980s the German economy was faced with structural changes
one of which has been technological changes. The union strategies focus
upon protection against an increase of work-load and stress, against
de-skilling, and on reduction of working time as a protection against
loss of jobs (Fürstenberg 1987). However, there existed no general policy
of job creation by reducing working time. A very important issue in
view of the introduction of new technologies has been job security. The
growing number of collective agreements containing provisions related
to the introduction of new technology demonstrates, according to some
experts, sound continuing flexibility in the West German model of industrial relations. As for the introduction of new technologies, German
trade unions have used their legal rights to information and consultation
in order to influence the terms under which new technologies have been
brought in.

The research programme for 'Humanization of Work Life' (now 'Work
and Technology') administered by the Federal Ministry of Research and
Technology is supported in principle by unions and employers. Many
action research projects have taken place within that framework. During
1977–87, there was a systematic increase in the rate of unemployment.
It was lowest (3.1 per cent) in 1980 and highest (9.2 per cent) in 1985—the
highest level since the 1930s.

In the Federal Republic of Germany, the major piece of legislation in
the industrial democracy area during 1976–86 was the 1976 Co-Determina-

tion Act. For more than a quarter of a century, the German Confederation of Trade Unions has been demanding equal representation of employees on the supervisory boards of companies in sectors other than iron, steel and mining industries. This demand was directed at firms of a certain size or with a certain financial turnover. It met with strong opposition from the German Employers' Confederation. A compromise was reached by the coalition government of the Social Democrats and Liberals. An Act was adopted, by a large majority, in the Federal Parliament which came into force in July 1976 (see Hanami and Monat 1988), and which relates to the supervisory boards of joint stock or limited companies and of limited partnerships employing more than 2,000 workers. The 1976 law provides that shareholders and employees are to be represented in equal number on the supervisory board, having a total of 12, 16, or 20 members according to the size of the enterprise. The supervisory board elects a chairman and a vice chairman from among its members by a majority of two-thirds of the total number of members of which it is required to be composed.

There are two main differences between the 1951 and 1976 laws. (1) Outside the 'Montan industries' (coal, steel, iron) at least one employee representative is nominated. (2) In impasse situations the chairman who is nominated by the shareholders has a casting vote (Fürstenberg 1987). The first election under the Act (in August 1978) concerned 484 firms, as against 600 to 650 which were expected to fall under the Act. The remainder had changed their legal status to one that was outside the purview of the Act (Streeck 1984: 402).

Amendments to the 1951 Co-Determination Act on parity-level representation for workers in the coal and steel industries were introduced in 1981 (the legislation was felt necessary in view of the Mannesmann steel and engineering firms which planned restructuring and attempted to take the company outside the scope of the legislation). The most important amendment was that any company with more than 1,000 workers predominantly concerned with coal, iron, or steel production must continue to apply parity board representation for another six years after it changes its production.

In 1980, the Federal Labour Court determined that overtime arrangements must be submitted for consent to the works council when the arrangement involves more than a single worker in the unit affected. The decision of the court on that matter was in conformity with the viewpoint of the unions.

In the Federal Republic of Germany, the main debates covered the reduction and 'flexibilization' of work-time, an end to the influx of foreign workers, and a trend towards more qualitative demands from the union side. One central demand was the revision of § 90/91 of the Works Constitution Law which stipulates that the representative body had the right of co-determination in the field of working conditions, but only if there is an offence against generally accepted findings in ergonomics.

The West German government finances many research projects which examine the relationship between working conditions and social consequences. Projects concerning industrial democracy also fall within this research area. The unions have made more qualitative demands during the decade under study and were about to decentralize their 'classical' centralized union policy. The emphasis in the field of industrial democracy concerns involving the workers and representative bodies in work-organizations before introducing new technology innovation. Probably as a result of the legal requirements of co-determination, a high level of employee representative involvement in issues related to technological change was found in the Federal Republic in a recent comparative survey conducted in Europe. Included in the survey were the United Kingdom, France, West Germany, Italy, and Denmark (Di Martino 1987). Employee representatives in Germany were found in this survey to be also the most satisfied with the amount of information given by the management regarding the introduction of new technology. They also found it most useful. Still, both employee representatives and managers 'felt that there were fewer positive outcomes resulting from involvement than their counterparts in other countries' (p. 10).

Finland

In Finland, the political situation has been quite stable during the period 1975–85. The country has been ruled by a coalition government since 1966, where the main partners have been the Social Democratic Party and the Centre Party backed by some smaller centre parties. This coalition prevailed until the 1987 parliamentary elections. It held such a majority that parliamentary opposition, as regards its size and effect, remained modest.

For twenty years, a dominant feature of Finnish political life was a spirit of consensus. During that period all questions and solutions arose from the ability to compete internationally and from a reasonable, placid incomes policy. The government was willing to negotiate with the labour-market partners with the intention of drawing them into consensus politics and away from opposition. A process of consultation with the trade unions and the employers on labour market issues, has characterized the Finnish political-economic system. This consensus-spirit policy has not changed even after the parliamentary election of 1987 when a coalition of conservatives, social democrats, and some small centre parties came into power.

The consensus-spirit principle has naturally greatly affected the economic performance of Finland. During the 1980s, the Finnish economy developed favourably and remained stable. The growth in GNP has been one of the highest among the OECD-countries and co-operation between employers, trade unions, and the government has created a relatively stable peace, especially in comparison with the 1960s and the early 1970s.

Industry and the service sectors began expanding at the same time. More of the population has gone straight from primary production into services in Finland than in any other country (Kauppinen 1987: 8). Rapid economic growth in the 1980s has put strong pressure on Finnish industry to develop high technology, training requirements have grown, and the gap between the qualifications for blue- and white-collar operations has narrowed. The first signs of slump due to the oil crisis came in 1975. Real earnings dropped in 1977, unemployment peaked at 7.3 per cent in 1978—the highest rate since the 1930s (it went gradually down to 5.4 per cent in 1986)-and became the main problem of the government. To promote recovery, the Finn currency was devalued (by a total of 17 per cent in 1977 and 1978), pay rises were postponed for six months, and industry was granted tax concessions. As a result the economy recovered and in 1980 it grew faster than in most OECD countries.

One of the ways by which Finnish managers have developed their operations more effectively has been by forming profit centres and granting supervisors more autonomy in managing them. Also, the very fast internationalization of Finnish firms during the last decade has had a favourable impact upon the economic performance of the country.

A modest two-year incomes policy agreement was signed in 1981 after the second oil crisis hit Finland. The incomes policy agreement for 1984–5 included pay indexation and shortening working hours. Also, a ninefold increase of fines was agreed in an effort to reduce the thousands of wildcat strikes that occurred annually in Finland. But academically trained unions abstained from signing the agreement and strikes by medical practitioners, teachers, and others were of very long duration. The 1986 agreement (for blue-collar employees) included, in addition to pay, a reduction in working time for 40-hour-a-week employees by 16 hours a year from 1987–9, and by 20 hours in 1990. Public sector employees went on strike for very long periods because of the pay lag in the growing public sector since 1970.

In the first half of the 1970s incomes policy succeeded in maintaining peace on the labour front, but recent experience has shown that incomes policy alone is an inadequate means of controlling demands. In the long run, the present system of incomes policy agreements may cause rigidity in negotiating procedures and impede the solution of specific sectorial problems unless it is continually adapted to changing circumstances. Since late 1980 there has been a growing pressure for decentralization of the bargaining process.

The previously mentioned consensual system which has developed in Finland had a great impact on the industrial relations system during 1976–86. This spirit was forced by the argument that international competition demand industrial peace. While the Finnish economy grew favourably, thanks greatly to the consensus-policy in the labour market, material goals became dominant among the people, which again decreased the earlier strong demands for industrial democracy and participation in enterprises.

A change in the workers' normative rights to participate took place in Finland in 1979. Workers' participation is based since then on the Co-operation Within Enterprises Act. It came into force on 1 July 1979. Before 1979, workers' possibilities to participate in enterprises were rather limited. The production committee system that prevailed for more than thirty years (adopted in 1946 and renewed in 1949) provided a forum for discussion and exchange of information only, and, therefore, its practical significance remained small. As a consequence of the democratization tendencies in society as a whole, the need for more democracy also in firms became pronounced. Lengthy negotiations began in the mid-1960s. Finally, in 1978 the negotiating parties on industrial relations, namely state, employers', and employees' organizations, were able to reach a sufficiently satisfactory agreement on the regulation of worker participation.

Parties to the co-operation according to the Cooperation Within Enterprises Act are the employer and the personnel of the company. Practical co-operation takes place either between individual employees and their superiors, or between the representative of the employer and the personnel. The purposes of the Act are to develop the functioning and the conditions of work in undertakings and to make co-operation between the management and the personnel more effective.

The scope of the Act is wide, covering decisions of varying strategic importance. The matters subject to co-operation are included in a vast catalogue (IDE 1981*a*: 97–8) which comprises matters having an essential influence on the position of personnel, essential changes in the functioning of the enterprise or a part thereof, the influence of such changes on the number of personnel in various occupations, sets of rules affecting the position of personnel, and questions pertaining to training, information, and social work. In most of the matters indicated, co-operation under the Act consists of consultation and information. Before a decision is taken on such a matter, the employer shall discuss the grounds, effects, and alternatives of the measure with the employees or personnel representatives concerned and give them the information necessary for the handling of the matter. After the required consultations, the decision—and the responsibility for it—rests with the employer (Suviranta 1987).

The required behaviour from the employers' side is consultation with the workers. So what is new here compared with the time of production committees? As stated earlier, those committees provided a forum for discussions and the exchange of information. There are at least two distinctions. First, according to the Cooperation Within Enterprises Act, participation is meant to be a continuing dialogue between the employer and the employees of a firm. No official forms are needed for this. Second, there are some items on which the workers have the final say. These are matters of a social character.

Since the Cooperation Within Enterprises Act came into force on 1 July 1979, public discussion in Finland about participation in enterprises has calmed down considerably. The reason for this 'silence' has not only been the above-mentioned law and its application law and its application to enterprises, but also several other general factors, of which we can briefly mention the following: the occupational structure of Finnish society has changed perhaps more rapidly than in other industrialized countries; the proportion of industrial blue-collar workers has declined, and especially the share of services has grown considerably within the labour force; and along with this change, the power of the conservative parties has grown.

With the rising standard of living, the goals of the individual at all societal levels have become more materialistic, leaving little room for ideological discussions concerning, e.g. industrial democracy and participation in enterprises. Also, the previously mentioned consensus policy in the labour market, international competition, and the strong emphasis on profitability in enterprises have lessened the 'political' demands concerning participation. On the other hand, we could say that participation has grown in the way that management increasingly uses workers and other employee groups on different joint projects, and many enterprises have voluntarily taken employees' representatives on to the board of directors and/or supervisory boards of enterprises.

In the old ideological sense, workers no longer see participation as an important question in enterprises. This came out clearly in a large survey which the Central Organization of Finnish Trade Unions conducted among its members. However, although participation is no longer a popular topic in general societal discussions, the Social Democratic Party took the development of working life and participation in enterprises as one of the official programme points into the coalition government. According to this government programme, a law was under preparation which would give the employees the right to have representatives on the supervisory boards of large enterprises. At the end of 1987 a state committee on 'New Forms of Industrial Democracy' suggested the creation of so-called employee investment funds in enterprises on a voluntary basis.

To summarize the main changes in the prevailing attitudes on participation we could say that during the period of 1977–87 among employees there was relatively little interest towards industrial democracy issues in enterprises. Among trade unions a new realism prevailed, as in Britain. The earlier sometimes heated discussions about the subject disappeared. There was, however, in practice considerable participation in enterprises at different levels, but it was not based on the ideological goals of industrial democracy, but rather on the material goals of increased productivity and profitability for the enterprise to succeed in (international) competition, and to ensure that workers will not lose their jobs and become unemployed.

Israel

In the 1980s, Israel has seen a swing to the Right, with successively Likud (Right) and then coalition governments. In 1977 the Likud vote was 33.4 per cent, and in 1981 this had risen to 37.1 per cent, but 1984 saw this fall to 33 per cent, and by 1988 to 31.8 per cent.

Important developments took place in Israeli government policy. In view of the growing rate of inflation, which in 1985 amounted to about 450 per cent, in July of that year the government initiated a new economic policy which was based on a tripartite agreement between the government, the Histadrut (the Labour Federation), and the Manufacturers Association (private sector). Such agreements had also taken place on an occasional basis in the past, but in 1985 the emergency situation called for a wider and deeper agreement between the three main factors of the industrial relations system at the national level. The results of this agreement (in the achievement of which the Labour Prime Minister took the leading role) were outstanding: the rate of inflation fell from 450 per cent per annum to 20 per cent per annum.

International economic competition, the increased number of multinational subsidiaries, especially in the high-tech industries, a relatively high rate of unemployment, the introduction of new technologies—all these and the other structural changes which characterize industrialized market economies have been witnessed in Israel for the decade under study. They were in existence even earlier, but during this decade they have undergone a process of intensification. At the same time immigrant absorption, the struggle against external enemies, and the shift towards a right-wing government (compared to the period before 1977) have pushed the subject of industrial democracy back from the forefront of public policies in Israel (Rosenstein, *et al.* 1987).

Until the late 1970s, collective bargaining in Israel took place at three levels: national, industry, and plant. During the last decade there has been a tendency, mainly under the pressure of the employers' association, to eliminate the industry (branch) level, and as a result many national unions have played but a minor role in the collective bargaining area. Negotiations between the employers and employees took place mainly at the national level, with supplementary negotiations at the company–plant level. Leaders of some national unions within the His- tadrut complained very bitterly about this situation. In some cases, such as the unions of engineers, technicians, and social science professionals there were very strong separatist expressions and organizational plans were made by them to leave the Histadrut. The leadership of the Histadrut was forced to allow these unions more autonomy and to enable them to negotiate directly with the employers. This opened the way to the decentralization of the collective bargaining process especially towards the sector (industry) level in Israel. In the traditional industries the process is still quite centralized.

As has been mentioned, there has been a strengthening of the tripartite agreement system since 1985 when the issues under discussion turned from lowering the inflation rate to economic growth, the establishment of new industrial enterprises, and the decrease of the rate of unemployment which peaked at 7.1 per cent in 1986 compared to 3.6 per cent in 1976. The closure of unprofitable industrial enterprises in the private sector and in the Labour Economy (enterprises owned by the Histadrut) has caused a great number of early retirements and lay-offs in recent years.

In the growing electronic industry in Israel's private sector, there has been a strong tendency to stay away from collective bargaining and to conclude individual agreements with employees. This was a relatively new phenomenon in Israel, where the general rate of unionization is around 80 per cent. The situation is quite peculiar in this respect, since a considerable percentage of employees in the privately owned high-tech enterprises are members of the Histadrut (membership is primary and not through specific unions), but since shop stewards committees most often do not exist at the company or plant levels of the privately owned electronic industries, these members of the Histadrut have no trade union representation and protection. The rate of personal (rather than collective agreements with senior managers and with specialists has increased since 1975 both in the private and government sectors.

The Israeli industrial relations system is still characterized by its high degree of organization in the labour market. The most meaningful bargaining takes place between the trade union section of the Histadrut on one hand and the private employers association on the other. In addition, the Histadrut negotiates with the government in its capacity as an employer. At the plant level, the most meaningful bodies which represented the employees *vis-à-vis* management during the 1976–86 decade were still the shop stewards committees. Joint productivity councils have spread from industrial enterprises into parts of the governmental administration. The joint management pattern within the Histadrut sector has been on a steady decline, whereas quality circles gained a growing popularity in management circles during the 1980s.

The Industrial Democracy issue in Israel has not been considered a matter requiring government action. During the 1980s the issue was not discussed as such in the Knesset (Israeli parliament) nor was it a matter for new legislation. In principle, Israel left industrial democracy issues in the hands of the Histadrut and the employers. The implementation of regulations (1977) concerning the representation of employees on the Boards of Directors of Government-owned industrial enterprises was discussed by the Finance Committee of the Knesset. The decision was to introduce such representatives in five Government-owned enterprises, but this has not been fully implemented. One should remember, however, that shop stewards' committees ('Workers' Committees' in Israel terms) are very widespread among Israeli organizations, including those which are state-owned.

In the 'Workers' Economy', especially in the industrial enterprises owned by the Histadrut, there have been in the last decade repeated formal declarations about the importance of workers' participation in management, but no new rules and regulations have been formulated in this area. In fact, during the last decade, the Histadrut has adopted a more pluralistic and less doctrinaire approach towards participation. This can be explained also by the continuous and severe economic problems which many Histadrut owned companies faced during the 1980s.

In 1979, the Employers' Association and the Histadrut (in its function as a trade union) renewed their agreement concerning the Joint Production Councils, which are based on a parity principle and in which decisions demand the majority of each of the two parties. These councils, which have spread during the last decade into state and municipal service organizations, are to be found mainly in industrial enterprises in the private sector, as well as in the state-owned and Histadrut-owned enterprises. Although the 1979 agreement specifies a long list of subjects (such as saving of raw material, quality improvement, technical training, etc.) which are to be discussed by the JPCs, studies indicate that their activities have most often concentrated on work methods and incentive payments, mostly in terms of norms and premiums (Rosenstein, *et al.* 1987).

Since the mid-1980s, there has been a growing interest in and introduction of quality circles in Israeli organizations. This applies to the private, government, and Histadrut (workers' economy) sectors. The introduction of quality circles has been usually initiated by management and was only seldom based on a formal agreement between the shop stewards' committee and management, although the shop stewards' committee was usually informed about the programme.

Industrial democracy did not seem to be an important issue in Israel in general. It has not become a public issue and has not played an important role in general political debates in the country. In the 1984 and 1988 elections, for example, it was hardly mentioned. During the 1989 elections to the Histadrut (Federation of Labour) convention reference was made to it by the Labour party leaders and by leaders of other left-wing parties. In the 1980s, the subject has often been discussed in Histadrut circles, but these discussions usually concerned the question of how to introduce meaningful participative structures within industrial enterprises and service organizations which are owned by the Histadrut itself. The general conception has been that the joint management schemes, which were formally adopted several times by the official bodies of the Histadrut since the 1960s, have not taken off as expected and, being clearly a representative (indirect) method of participation, it has not improved the identification of the individual employee with the organization. As a result of this disappointment there has been, in the later 1980s, a growing interest in a more pluralistic approach to participation.

Within the Histadrut there has also been a growing interest in and implementation of workers' representatives at the board of directors' level and growing attention has been paid again to the idea of financial participation in the Histadrut sector. In the early 1980s, the translation of the industrial democracy concept within the Histadrut sector was implemented by means of general employee meetings as well as by welfare and social activity.

All these attempts can be seen as a continuous search by the Histadrut for a valid scheme, or schemes, of participation. Such a search has been in existence for a long time. Recently, the Industrial Democracy section of the Histadrut, together with the fast developing Histadrut College, initiated a training programme in Participative Management.

The Netherlands

The Netherlands cabinet, made up of Christian Democrats and Liberals, in office since 1982 (after a coalition which also included the Labour Party fell apart), was less interested in regulating industrial relations and introducing industrial democracy than its predecessors. It pursued a 'no-nonsense policy' to stimulate the economy by cutting back government spending and by 'liberating' trade and industry from state intervention, etc. However, the government, as the country's biggest employer and trendsetter for wage policies in the public sector, has found it hard to reduce its substantial role in the industrial relations system. Since 1989 the Netherlands has gained a Christian-Socialist cabinet, but that has not changed the picture drastically yet.

For many years Dutch industrial relations were dominated by a centralized approach, with government playing an influential role in a wide range of policy areas. Legislation dealing with workers' participation in decision-making, as is argued by Ramondt (1987), may be considered part of that tradition. An Act regulating co-determination in companies with between 35 and 100 employees has been in effect since 1982. It should be noticed at the same time that from the beginning of the 1970s management and trade unions 'became less willing to accommodate themselves to a centralized approach and instead responded to pressure from their rank and file' (ibid.: 78). In the Netherlands, initiatives to increase the opportunities for participation among workers have come from the companies, the trade unions, and the academic world. Attention is being paid in recent years to overcome the rather pluralistic pattern and the built-in rivalries among participatory forums.

Many unions in the Netherlands have been severely weakened by loss of members and of bargaining-power. There is a trend towards fragmentation and/or decentralization of the once strongly centralized and well-disciplined Industrial Relations system in the Netherlands. Prominent figures from the employers' side and from politics have argued in favour of a reduced role for the unions in the annual or bi-annual round of industry-wide bargaining. Some say that the unions ought to restrict themselves to negotiating the general outlines of a collective agreement and leave further details to bargaining at the firm level between management and works council. Others even envisage a future in which unions can be dispensed with altogether.

Recent evidence (Pool *et al.* 1988) shows that in spite of set-backs, such as the weakening of the union movement, higher unemployment, and the apparent 'de-democratization' trend in the private sector and in public life, the general level of participation, both direct and indirect, is certainly not lower, and perhaps even a bit higher in the 1980s than ten years ago in the Netherlands. Representation by a works council at the level of the firm, and consultation by employers at the shop-floor level have become institutionalized to such an extent as to become a viable part of normal working life.

In the Netherlands, claims Albeda (1984), trade unions are well known for their co-operative attitude. However, the attempts made by various cabinets to establish some form of 'social contract' did not generally meet with success. In some cases, the yearly rounds of central collective bargaining set the boundaries for the decentralized bargaining in trade and industry.

In the end of the 1970s and by the beginning of the 1980s, Dutch governments have quite often imposed wage freezes on the trade unions and the employers, in spite of the evaluation that, from a political point of view, the advantages of voluntary agreements over wage control are important. A few firms in the Netherlands (public utilities, petrochemical sector) reduced the average working week to 33.6 hours in the early 1980s. Clearly, the central agreement on the reduction of working time leaves room for decentralized implementation (Albeda 1984).

The Works Council Act of 1971 in the Netherlands was amended in 1979 and again in 1982. The first piece of legislation is popularly known as the Works Council Act of 1979 (WCA 79) and the second one as the '100-law'. In 1980, a Work Environment Act was passed which also contains a number of clauses having to do with Industrial Democracy. In all three cases, one can notice a sort of 'cultural lag' or 'legislative lag', in the sense that the legislation in question was prepared in the early 1970s and reflects the concerns and 'mood' of those days, but became enacted and had to be implemented in different political and economic circumstances and under the aegis of quite another *Zeitgeist*.

WCA 79

This change in the law regarding works councils aimed at making councils in work organizations of 100 or more employees (*a*) more independent (of the employer) and (*b*) more powerful. As to (*a*), the top manager no longer chairs the meetings: elected councillors now nominate one of themselves as chairman of the council. The council meets regularly without any management representatives being present, while separate 'consultative sessions' are held to advise the management and to obtain information from it. As to (*b*), WCA 79, as compared to WCA 71, has increased the number of issues on which the management has to take the advice of its council. Furthermore, its co-determination rights (that is, decisions on which management has to obtain the consent of its council) were extended.

100-Law

In 1981, the range of organizations for which a council is obligatory was extended to all work organizations. In the case of establishments with between 35 and 100 employees there is now a council with (in some respects) fewer powers than in organizations of 100 +, while the prescribed procedures are a bit simpler. The law stipulates for work organizations of between 10 and 35 employees that the owner or manager has to convene the work-force twice a year to supply them with information, or more frequently when requested by 25 per cent of the work-force, giving the reasons. This meeting can advise him if he intends to take decisions affecting their position, their work, their working circumstances, or their conditions of employment. Actually, the agenda proposed by either side may deal with all subjects concerning the life of the undertaking.

The 1980 Work Environment Act

This law, which concerns the health, safety, and well-being of employees in the Netherlands, is modelled to some extent on the Norwegian Work Environment Act of 1977 and was also influenced by similar legislation in Britain and by the German government programme of 1974 to further the 'humanization of working life'. However, the implementation of this law made a slow start in 1983, and only a small number of its provisions and prescriptions have been realized. Among the cases for this delay can be mentioned:

- the continuing need for decreasing expenditure by government;
- government efforts at deregulation (the present Centre–Right Cabinet has already announced its intention to revise this law);
- increased doubts on the part of the Employers'-front (and right-wing politicians) with respect to the desirability of striving for 'well-being' of employees by means of legislation;
- decreased attention to 'quality of working life' issues on the part of unions, given the severity of the 'quality of work' problems.

In general, the impact on industrial democracy of this last Act has so far been rather slight. Perhaps here and there a small effect on the position of works councils might be noticeable. The law in question contains provision for the introduction of a committee of representatives from the workers' side and from management to establish policies with respect to health, safety, and well-being, but in case there is a works council, this body is legally entitled to function as such a committee. In other words, the Dutch Work Environment law in principle enhances the scope of operation of the works councils.

In the Netherlands, the issue of macro-level participation has continued to occupy the attention of the government, unions, and employers during the late 1970s and the 1980s, despite the lack of success in institutionalizing a social contract pattern. Unemployment became 'the social evil that concerned trade unions, employers and government alike. As a consequence, although complete consensus was out of reach, partial agreement was possible' (Albeda 1987: 15). Evidence for such agreement at the macro-level are various formal agreements which were concluded during the 1980s on issues such as economic recovery, shortening of working hours (with the intention of creating employment), a programme of training and retraining of unemployed workers, and the intensified development of training within the enterprise in general.

At the enterprise level, the works councils have in recent years been occupying a growing central position in the Dutch system of organizational democracy. They have also become more powerful institutions in terms of their influence on strategic managerial decisions. In general they have developed into an established mature institution (Teulings

1987). The revision of the law on works councils, which was im-plemented in 1979, can explain to a great extent the strengthening of the Dutch works councils, which in all matters of collective, social, and personnel policy have co-determination rights. It can be assumed that the strengthened status of the works councils in the Netherlands during the last decade, and the existence of very influential councils which sometimes use radical strategies have attracted public opinion and the parties involved in the enterprise to this potentially effective method of industrial democracy at the enterprise level.

Norway

The election of 1981 in Norway resulted in a change of government to the Right. The Conservative-Centre coalition maintained power (on a minority basis) in the election of 1985, but was forced to (or decided to) resign in May 1986. The Labour Party headed a minority government, tolerated by the Centre until the 1989 election, when a new Centre–Right government came into power.

The 1981 elections introduced an important shift in the political history of Norway. Since 1927 the Labour Party alone has held a majority of votes in every single Storting election. The party first came to power on a lasting basis in 1935, and has stayed in power for more than four decades. 'It is hardly surprising therefore', claims Lafferty (1990: 80), 'that the Norwegian Labour Party has come to be considered as the "natural" instrument of government in Norway. With the exception of its sister-party in Sweden, no other labour-based, quasi-socialist party can claim such a status within the Western sphere.'

The turn to the right has resulted in several 'reversals' in previous labour policies and institutions. For example, the system of proportional representation in the governing bodies of the commercial banks was altered so that the majority was returned to the shareholders. (The built-in majority had previously been in the direction of the employees and politically appointed representatives.) Savings banks continue with a majority in the hands of the employees and politically appointed representatives.

During the decade under study, there has been a tendency towards 'liberalization' of important economic areas in the Norwegian economy. The financial, stock, and housing markets have all been moderately deregulated and there has been a change in 'mood' in the direction of greater sympathy for management-related values.

Together with Sweden, the rate of unemployment in Norway has been the lowest of the OECD countries during the 1976–86 decade. At its highest, the rate in 1983 was 3.4 per cent in Norway and 3.5 per cent in Sweden. The Norwegian and the Swedes have basically preferred inflation when pressed to choose between inflation and unemployment (Lafferty 1988). This changed in the mid-1980s, however, when the Labour government introduced strict austerity measures to bring inflation under control.

The first Conservative government, which came into power in 1987, withdrew a new law passed by the Labour Government which would have provided for worker representation on special governing boards in the public sector (where roughly one-third of all Norwegian employees are now engaged). The withdrawal elicited a political demonstration strike against the government by employees in the public sector, and the issue was later turned over to the bargaining table where it has since been resolved.

One of the most important new features in Norwegian collective bargaining has been the introduction of a supplementary agreement to the Basic Agreement between the employers (NAF) and the central labour organization (LO) in 1982. The agreement is mainly concerned with the development of work organization in the firm, with stipulations as to 'mapping conferences', 'job design projects', and 'development grants' (for both management and labour: up to two years to concentrate on developmental work and job qualification). Together with other agreements and laws, this agreement indicates a new trend towards placing greater importance on local organizational development and the building up of a national infrastructure to initiate and support such work. There are at present approximately 300 local projects of this type in progress. In 1987, it was decided to establish a new Center for a Better Work Life, with a proposed budget of 30 million Norwegian Crowns (4.5 million dollars).

In 1980, a new Basic Agreement came into effect between the state and major employee organizations in the public sector (the LO, YS ('functionaries')), AF ('academicians', i.e. those with an academic education), and teachers. Part Two of this agreement is a 'framework agreement' devoted mainly to 'co-determination'. The agreement provides guidelines for the negotiation of local agreements as to the involvement of worker representatives in ongoing decision-making. Similar arrangements have been integrated into basic agreements for local government employees and further provisions at the level of the municipality have also been worked out for the establishment of 'Administrative Councils' where public employees are to be given representation over working conditions and personnel policies.

Of further interest in principle, if not necessarily in practice, was an amendment to the Norwegian Constitution in 1980 which added to the existing 'right to work' paragraph that: 'More explicit decisions as to the employee's right to co-determination at work will be determined by law' (para. 110). Although highly cryptic in formulation, the amendment served to legitimize this particular aspect of the Norwegian political culture.

It should also be mentioned here that Norway has had a wide-ranging 'Law on Equality between the Sexes' since 1978. There are several sections of this law with direct relevance to work life, including sections on 'equality of hiring', 'equal wages for work of equal value', and minimum requirements for gender representation on all official boards and committees. Both Norway and Sweden are characterized by a high degree of organization in the labour-market. About 60 per cent of the employees in Norway and more than 75 per cent in Sweden are union members. The chief actors in the labour-market on both sides are large federations.

The single most important Act introduced during the last decade in Norway in relation to Industrial Democracy is the Work Environment Act of 1977. The Act specified different strategies, including programmes for employee empowerment and firm development. The intention of the legislation was to create a framework whereby those who are actually affected by environmental problems could gain a better understanding of them, and at the same time develop specific organizational means for defining, controlling, and solving work-environment problems. It was expected that the decentralization and democratization of the area would also promote greater efficiency in solving these problems (see Lafferty 1984). The Work Environment Act represents to some extent a break with legal traditions in the field of health and safety in that it merged ideas about worker participation with ideas about health and safety in an attempt to bring worker participation to bear on the issue of improving the work environment (Gustavsen 1983: 545; Gustavsen and Hunnius 1981). The 1977 Act stipulates, for example, that 'the individual employee's opportunity for self-determination and professional responsibility shall be taken into consideration when planning and arranging work' or that 'efforts shall be made to arrange the work so as to provide possibilities for variation and for contact with others for connection between individual job assignments and for employees to keep themselves informed about production requirements and results'. Also, the employees and their elected union representatives are to be informed about the systems employed for planning and effecting work and about planned changes in such systems. Moreover, they shall be given the necessary training to enable them to learn these systems and shall take part in planning them.

Towards the end of the 1970s the issue of Industrial Democracy came up again in the Labour Movement (which is the normal cycle—once every ten years). A committee composed by the Labour Movement (Union plus Labour Party) proposed: (1) 50 per cent employee representation at the board level (an expansion from the current 33 per cent), and (2) the development of a new kind of legislation which should

secure participation in the decision-making process at all stages of preparation before formal final decision. The proposal was read by the Employers' Federation as a demand for a bureaucratic system in each
enterprise whereby decision-making should follow a particular pattern
of committees or meetings in which the unions were represented and
could exert influence. These suggestions met with strong opposition
from the Norwegian Employers' Confederation.

A commission was later appointed by the Labour government to look
into the question of further democratization in the private sector. It was
asked to pinpoint measures which in addition to being democratic
would also promote productivity. A unanimous recommendation for a
national programme to promote participative forms of organization and
management in order to create productivity and change came out in
1984. The commission actually decided to leave for the time being the
controversial issue of increased worker share by means of seats in the
boardroom. Thus the participation issue was perceived by the commission as an effective means for improving productivity rather than as
a social end in itself.

In 1987 the government and labour-market organizations agreed jointly to finance a new five-year programme, which was to include both the
private and public sectors. A new centre, SBA, was created in 1988 to
carry out that task.

The two most important debates of the period 1976–86 in Norway have
probably been those related to the introduction of the Work Environment Act of 1977 and the extensive media debate in connection with the
so-called Skytøen Report of 1980 on the 'Future Development of Work-
place Democracy'. The main tensions in the debate on the Work
Environment Act had to do with the predicted costs (mainly by the
employers) of the reform. The main tensions in the debate of the Skytøen
Report focused on the proposal by the committee for 50 : 50 representation on governing bodies.

The first half of the period was especially marked by a tendency to
treat co-determination as a basic right. During the second half, there has
been a slight shift in the direction of focusing on participation as a
productive resource: 'productive' both with regard to traditional cost
reduction, but also in relation to mobilization of new resources and
innovation in different fields.

The labour union side to a large extent realized that centrally imposed
laws and other rules will not contribute to the solving of the major
economic problem, namely, how to remain competitive in increasingly
international markets. This shift in thinking came through the Commission on Industrial Democracy, which delivered its report in 1985. Its
recommendations were accepted by all labour-market organizations and
political parties. The report called for measures which would contribute

towards increased productivity and change in the individual enterprise, i.e. enhanced participation in the daily work situation. Its recommendation for a national programme for promoting direct participation jointly sponsored by all social partners was unanimously accepted by the Trade Union Congress in 1987 and the programme started in 1988 (Qvale personal communication). Thus, a perceived need for rapid economic/market changes tended to give cross-political agreement about the need for new strategies. So the Industrial Democracy issue has shifted in the late 1980s from the realm of workers' rights and welfare towards productivity/industrial policy. In the discussions there is relatively little talk about Industrial Democracy in itself, while the focus is on organizational and individual competence, commitment, flexibility, etc., and direct participation by the government through legislation goes down.

A great deal of the future debate will depend on the role played by the new Centre for a Better Working Life. Given the proposed size of the budget and the relatively limited resources otherwise in the Norwegian environment, much of the future discussion will originate here. A further source of influence will be the Labour-supported research organization, FAFO ('The Labour Movement's Centre for Research, Fact-finding, and Documentation').

Sweden

After a forty-four-year-long Social Democratic rule in Sweden (some periods in coalitions with bourgeois parties) a Centre–Conservative coalition came into power in 1976. In various constellations, the bourgeois parties stayed on until 1982, when Social Democratic minority government supported by the Communists took over. The regime of the three bourgeois parties was dominated by debates over the future of nuclear power. Owing to the internal debate concerning the energy question, the bourgeois government accomplished very little in other areas. They did not then cut down the excessive Swedish taxation rate (highest in the world—more than 50 per cent of GNP in taxes) and they did not cut down on government spending. Quite the contrary: they expanded government subsidies to failing industries. The budget became severely underbalanced and Sweden's foreign debt exploded.

Since the Social Democrats returned to power in 1982, their main concern has been to stabilize the economy. Their first measure was to increase the international competitiveness of Swedish industry by devaluing the currency by 16 per cent. Thereafter the expansion of public expenditure has been restricted. Taxes have also been reduced recently.

During the 1970s and 1980s, the economic growth of Sweden has been around the average for the richer industrialized nations inside the OECD. Inflation has been high and the income of the typical household decreased up to 1984. However, two important aspects of the economy have been successful. One is that employment has been kept high, with unemployment around 3 per cent, or lower. Recently, the tendency has been toward over-demand for labour in certain areas. The other aspect is that a restructuring of Swedish industry has taken place. Three major sectors have been affected: the shipbuilding industry has disappeared; steel and forestry have undergone a thorough restructuring with un- profitable units being closed; and the car industry has been very suc- cessful, becoming the country's most important export income-earner, mainly from sales on the US market.

'Over the past decade, there have been so many departures from the long-standing features of the Swedish industrial relations system as to suggest that the "Swedish model" of industrial relations was being replaced by a system differing significantly in its structure and mode of operation' (Martin 1987: 93). The Swedish model was characterized by having relatively few, well-organized and strong employers' associ- ations and unions. Moreover, the unions had a positive attitude toward rationalization and 'rely upon the government to pursue an active la- bour market policy in order to absorb technological and structural un- employment' (Hammarstrom 1987). The Swedish model has come under increased strain since the early 1970s, and especially since 1976, as the political and economic scene changed when the Social Democratic gov- ernment came to an end. The employers strongly resisted the radical demands of the unions for economic and industrial democracy. The demands for economic democracy (in the form of Wage Earner funds) were strongly opposed by the non-Socialist political parties as well as by the employers association, SAF, whereas the bourgeois parties stood behind the new industrial relations Laws.

Some commentators claimed that the Swedish model, with its spirit of co-operation, ended symbolically with the big strike of 1980 which was met by an employer lock-out of 80 per cent of the work-force. Another contribution to the probably temporary weakening of the traditional model was the intervening of the government in the pay determination process in 1980. However, the pay settlements in 1981 and 1983 were made without disputes, and during 1983 and 1984 agreements were reached without the help of mediators. In the Swedish political debate, incomes policy has long been a term with negative overtones. The tradi- tional Swedish model was based on the assumption that the employers and the unions assume responsibility for industrial peace and with wage structure which is compatible with a balanced national economy. But with the intervention of the government in the wage negotiations during the 1980s, this concept began to disintegrate (see Elvande 1987).

In the 1980s, Sweden has experienced a new element in its industrial relations; it is the move towards decentralized bargaining which started in 1983 upon the initiative of the employers as the Engineering Employers' Confederation reached an agreement with its counterpart unions outside the central round of negotiation. In 1984 the LO (trade union federation) declared that centralized bargaining was no longer possible and industry-wide bargaining was introduced throughout the private sector (Hammarstrom 1987). As a rule, Swedish unions have sympathized with economic rationalization and technological development (see Hammarstrom 1987).

The debate in Sweden in relation to industrial democracy has concentrated on two areas. One is work organization and the individual's influence over his job (often associated with the socio-technical approach). The other has been union influence over top management decision by means of collective bargaining and company board representation (see Long 1986; Hammarstrom 1987).

The concept of economic democracy in Sweden—which includes the idea of profit-sharing and collective ownership—was a topic for public debate in Sweden from 1971. The radical proposal for wage earners' funds (the Meidner Plan) was submitted in 1975 and in 1983 the new Social Democratic party introduced a diluted version of the original proposal. The whole issue of economic democracy was a subject of fierce disagreement between the LO and the private employers during the 1970s and 1980s.

In 1977, the Swedish Co-determination at Work Act (MBL) replaced a number of old agreements, and became the legal framework for industrial democracy. This act stipulates that the employer has a duty to consult with the unions before any important decision on major changes (which range from reorganization to the introduction of new technologies) or any decision that affects an individual union member could be taken. Management is not obliged to reach agreement, but it has to allow time for unions to investigate the matter and negotiate at either local or central level before it implements decisions. The law did not specify exactly how the consultation should be carried out but left it to the parties in the labour-market to agree about the forms of labour participation. It proved to be very difficult for the parties in the big private sector to reach agreement on these procedures. Therefore, co-determination agreements were not entered until 1981, or later. In the mean time, friction was generated between the parties—to which a great number of lawsuits bear witness. The result was a good deal of disappointment among union activists when they realized that the new law did not really provide them with any greater degree of power than before. Eventually, the new forms of collaboration between management and labour were institutionalized and now seem to work rather smoothly. Co-determination has become incorporated into the management structure of Swedish firms. By law, two local union-based directors can belong to the board of most private companies which employ at least twenty-five people—a right which is mainly used in large and medium-sized companies (Hammarstrom 1987).

The great industrial relations issue during the first part of the 1980s has been the 'wage-earners' funds'. The suggestion for the establishment of the funds came from the blue-collar confederation of unions. According to this suggestion, a share of the profits of privately owned companies should be channelled to special funds managed by people appointed by the unions. The funds should be used to buy up shares in the companies. This suggestion became a big embarrassment for the Social Democratic leadership, which did not like the idea. However, several wage-earners' funds have eventually been set up. They get their money from an extra tax put on all wages and which has to be paid by all the employers. In addition, all companies that reach a certain level of profitability have to pay part of their profits to the funds. The funds have been buying up shares on the stock market, in which they are one of the most important actors. However, the law specifies that the funds have to discontinue their activities after fifteen years in operation. Critics claim that the Swedish wage-earner funds are in fact a new method for the gradual socialization of the economy by the government.

On the whole, the funds have not been of much consequence for workers in individual firms. However, they represent one further step in the concentration of ownership of industry in the hands of institutional owners who do not get much involved in the management of companies in which they own shares.

The question of industrial democracy and workers' participation has lost much of its importance during the 1980s. The question of how Swedish industry could meet foreign competitors has been prominent. In this connection, an agreement has been reached between the employers and the labour side about co-operating in finding good ways for incorporating new technology in production.

The main issue for the labour side has, however, been wages. The union for the municipality workers has replaced the metal workers' union as the largest trade union in Sweden. Since public employees can threaten to strike without risking their employers' becoming bankrupt, their wages have increased at a much faster rate than those of industrial workers.

In Sweden, the introduction of the Act on Co-Determination at Work in 1977 and other laws which aimed at a reform of working life has been controversial between the labour-market parties but not so much among the diverse political parties. It was passed with a big majority in parliament. The unions expected that the reforms would improve the work environment, increase job satisfaction, and in general enable 'better control for individuals over their daily life at work and a stronger say for the local unions in the development of the enterprises in which their members work' (Hammarstrom 1987: 109). On the other hand, the legal changes met with strong opposition from the employers. They would have preferred legislation to promote the involvement of the individual employee rather than strengthen union activity. They feared that the new Act on Co-Determination at Work would result in higher costs, inefficiency, and make the decision-making process in the enterprises less effective. Some experts believe that the impact of the reforms was quite mild, which made the leadership of the unions feel disillusioned and disappointed, while most of the fears of the employers have not materialized (Haas 1983; Sandberg 1984). However, in 1982 worsening economic conditions prompted employers and unions to reach an agreement on efficiency and participation (known in Sweden as the 'development agreement'). There has been a renewed interest in Sweden in job-level experiments, which came as a result of the unions' disillusionment with the indirect and legally based participation methods of the late 1970s (see Long 1986). These experiments were often related to plant-level economic pressures and the need effectively to absorb new technologies.

The Work Environment Fund which is supporting research on job-related issues, supports the well-known Swedish Centre for Working Life which was established in 1977 in order to promote quality of working life experimentation on a very wide range. This large centre is mainly controlled by labour, although it is financed from levies on employers. It seems to exemplify the positive attitudes of the two partners towards the development of a participative approach for reaching both economic development of the firm and a high level of working life quality. This re-emphasis on collaborative work-place reforms in Sweden and other European countries should be seen against the background of the difficult economic conditions which prevailed in Europe during the early and mid-1980s (see Long and Warner 1984). On the whole, industrial democracy was a focal point of debate in Sweden during the 1970s, but in the 1980s it was replaced by the debate on new technology and economic competitiveness. This paved the way towards the collaborative work-place reforms based on experimentation.

United Kingdom

Following the general elections of 1979, in the United Kingdom the Conservative government rejected much of the post-war consensus on economic policy. The reduction of inflation through monetarist policies was accorded a higher priority than the maintenance of full employment. Moreover, the Conservatives argued that the unions had become too powerful and that legislation was needed to shift the 'balance of power' in industrial relations (Bamber & Snape 1987).

Consequently, the last decade has witnessed substantial change including major pieces of legislation, new working practices, and widespread debate about the role of trade unions. Major pieces of legislation have changed the law on the conduct of disputes, the use of the closed shop, and the internal operation of trade unions. Acts of 1980, 1982, and 1984 have altered the conditions under which industrial action is lawful by, for example, narrowing the definition of a trade dispute, requiring a secret ballot before official industrial action, and outlawing certain kinds of secondary action. In the light of legal and managerial changes, trade unions have been on the defensive but they have not been destroyed. Clearly, they have to face major challenges in coming to terms with legal and employer-led initiatives (for a more detailed discussion see Edwards & Sisson 1989). Some observers even see unions moving towards an 'enterprise unionism' in which the focus of concern is the individual company (Brown 1983). Clearly, the Conservative government in the United Kingdom during the 1980s has rejected the idea that representative participation, in addition to collective bargaining, is in principle a good idea. This attitude can be deduced from the fact that the participation idea has not been supported by legislation or by governmental agencies. Actually Mrs Thatcher had herself condemned as 'Marxist' plans to put workers on the boards of companies, and officials at the Department of Trade and Industry have warned the Commission of the European Community that they will challenge any harmonization of such an arrangement in the European Court (see *Independent* (22 Aug. 1989: 3)).

Since the election of successive Thatcher administrations from the late 1970s, a great deal has changed on the industrial relations scene in the United Kingdom. A number of significant factors can be noted. First, the change in the economic environment has had a considerable restraining influence on the industrial relations system. As unemployment has risen, the incidence of strikes has been reduced. Fear of the dole queue has also helped to slow down wage increases in a number of industries. Together with high interest rates, this has put pressure on the private sector, while the public sector has been affected by cash constraints on its expenditure and therefore its pay settlements. The fall in manufacturing employment due to the recession has very much undermined trade union membership in that sphere, although public sector unionism has been relatively less affected. In all, unionization has fallen from a peak of around 55 per cent in the mid-1970s, to something more near 45 per cent in the mid-1980s (see Roberts 1985), and possibly less subsequently. Unemployment rose from 6.2 per cent in 1977 to 11.9 per cent in 1986.

Since May 1979, when the swing to the political Right started, several changes have been made in the legal framework of trade unions. There have been changes in laws affecting the closed-shop, lawful picketing, and so on.

The recession subsided by the middle of the 1980s, 1986 being the year of the 'consumer boom', with the UK having the fastest economic growth rate in Europe, although having fallen behind in absolute terms over the decade.

Governments in most European countries tried to promote industrial democracy, but this has not been the case in the UK in the 1980s. At least, there have been fewer channels in Britain to do it than in most other Western European countries (see also Bamber & Snape 1987).

An important factor which has constrained industrial relations behaviour in the United Kingdom has been the Conservative administration's attempt to increase regulation of industrial behaviour by law, as noted earlier. Since 1979, several new laws have been introduced to make trade unions act 'more responsibly'. In most cases, strike-ballots are now necessary before industrial action can proceed. Another law has been brought in to introduce greater union democracy, thus allegedly increasing the influence of 'moderate' rank-and-file members. The growth in the closed-shop was blocked by the passing of the Employment Act of 1980, making it difficult for unions to win new closed-shop agreements. The 1982 Act, which came into effect in 1984, requires 80 per cent votes in favour from the membership to sign such deals. Another law regarding picketing, limiting action to the specific site of the dispute, has been brought in as part of this legislative package, with secondary picketing declared unlawful.

Public opinion polls had for some time reflected hostility to organized labour as having too much power, and the miners' dispute, which began in March 1984, did not enhance the overall image of the trade unions, owing to the public's perception of picket-line violence. However, since 1987, this image has somewhat improved. The defeat of the National Union of Miners in that protracted dispute represented a watershed in British industrial relations, as it appeared to vindicate the government's tough stance *vis-à-vis* the purported influence of militants in the labour movement.

While many factors have constrained rank-and-file behaviour, the role of shop stewards remained relatively important. Industrial disputes, even at national level, persisted. White-collar dissatisfaction, as exemplified in the drawn-out teachers' dispute of 1986/7, revealed public-sector union militancy exacerbated by government intransigence. More generally, according to one recent evaluation, 'provisions on balloting in disputes and on the tactics which may be deployed may have encouraged a constitutional trade unionism and help to marginalize the tradition of militant industrial action' (Edwards and Sisson 1989: 5). Estimates are that whichever party is in government the law will probably continue to play a key role in industrial relations in the United Kingdom, and the trend away from the British way of 'voluntarism' will continue. Also, the employers will probably retain much of the initiative in industrial relations system in the foreseeable future (Bamber & Snape 1987).

On the industrial democracy front in the United Kingdom, political and economic factors have not sustained a favourable climate for new developments to surface, let alone flourish. Nevertheless, an extension of profit-sharing, particularly in the service sector, has been noted backed up as it is by legislative provision (in the 1978, 1980, and 1984 Finance Acts). Furthermore, some expansion in the number of worker co-operatives has been visible. Indeed, the present government's legislation now requires each company to say something about its contribution to employee consultation in its annual report. Some experiments in the job design area have continued, but with none of the prominence seen in the 1970s. Trade union involvement continues, but in most cases this does not proceed beyond the consultation level (see Daniel 1987). Only a change of government would lead to any substantive implementation of industrial democracy proposals.

At the enterprise level, research data in the early 1980s revealed that among shop stewards there was a general and high degree of faith in the legitimacy and potential of industrial democracy. This, however, was not the case with the managers, most of whom have discerned a much more critical attitude towards it (Ursell 1983). A more recent report on involving employees in Britain concludes its series of empirical findings by recommending managements to promote involvement, consultation, and attention to job design at all levels of the organization (Webbs 1989).

Yugoslavia

From having a strong political personality as leader, Yugoslavia has switched to a model of collective presidency. During the 1970s and 1980s, individual politicians were elected to different offices for short periods of time (1–2 years), resulting perhaps in an increased number of lower-profile politicians and a more open conflict of interests between different regions in the country and groups within the government and the League of Communists. Alternative strategies for development and change of the political system (including a multi-party system) were very actively discussed and reported in the press. Economic and political differences between different regions increased dramatically and they were openly articulated and defined as the basis for different political and economic interests. In the 1980s Yugoslavia has experienced a rapid and growing economic malaise. This decade has brought recession—personal incomes rose in money terms but in view of the rapidly growing inflation (estimated as high as 2,500 per cent in late 1989), standard of living has fallen. Thus the real net personal income per worker in the productive social sector fell during 1979–85 by 24.9 per cent, and gross fixed investment by 37.2 per cent. The balance of payment deteriorated and there was a drastic rise in foreign indebtedness (see Warner 1990; Laydall 1989). Unemployment grew steadily during 1977–87 and reached a record of 14.1 per cent in 1986, the highest among the IDE countries and one of the highest unemployment rates in Europe.

The Yugoslav governments in the late 1980s adopted a policy of moving to a market economy as the answer to the countries with economic problems. But the fear of the market solution still seemed to persist among the leadership of the country.

In addition to the worsening economic conditions during the decade under study Yugoslavia suffered from threats to its federal unity. Also, severe ethnic tensions began to shake the social and political setting of Yugoslavia.

Self-management in Yugoslavia has long been conceived by Yugoslavs as a unique social institution characterizing Yugoslav Communism and distinguishing it from the centralized Soviet economic and management model. However, as the functioning of the economy deteriorated to a threatening extent the structural weaknesses of the self-management system became more and more evident. In the past the integrative role of workers' councils may have prevailed, 'but as soon as economic conditions deteriorated beyond the point of tolerability, the case for an adversarial [rather than the harmonious self-management system] industrial relations system became more convincing' (Warner 1990).

From 1976 to 1987 there were important changes in the Yugoslav industrial relations system. Trade unions continued to perform mainly an educational function

endeavouring to raise the level of understanding and social consciousness of workers so that they may effectively direct and control the entire process of maintenance and development of society as a whole . . . The role of the unions is inducing individual workers to identify with the organizations of associated labour in which they work . . . every aspect of their activities serves the purpose of strengthening social cohesion. (Pasić, Grozdanić, and Radević 1982)

It is clear from the above quotation that the unions were previously not expected to adopt an adversary role within the self-managed organization *vis-à-vis* the management. The basic model of the Yugoslav organization is an integrative one. Thus, the unions participated in organizations of associated labour in the entire decision-making process, including the workers' councils. In view of the fact that the union sometimes has no real influence on its members' thinking and decisions, efforts have been made in the 1980s to develop a more democratic approach within the unions to allow for criticism and new free confrontation of ideas (Pasić *et al.* 1982: 172). At the national level the government was required to consult the trade unions on matters of social policy.

The most important change in Yugoslav system has been an attempt to increase centralization of the economic decision-making, while maintaining the existing decentralization of the political system. These changes have been very recent, most of them occurring in the late 1980s.

The Law of Associated Labour (1974) both increased regional economic autonomy and established the so-called basic organizations of associated labour (BOALs)—a form of decentralization within the enterprise itself. After ten years of experience with this scheme, the main problem that emerged was a lack of co-ordination of economic decision-making on the national (federal) level, and because of that, increased difficulties in dealing with foreign partners and international financial institutions. On the enterprise level, individual BOALs have acted as separate firms, complete with separate accounting, and have made contracts with outside partners. In the 'internal market' BOALs of one firm competed with other firms on an equal footing for a contract within their own enterprise. The accounting and administration became very complicated and co-ordination on the enterprise level complex and sensitive.

In Yugoslavia, the period between 1977 and 1987 increasingly became a time of critical evaluation of self-management, which was blamed for a lengthy decision-making process in industry and lower efficiency. With increased economic difficulties and higher unemployment, the demand for increased democratization of decision-making began to drop from the focus of interest.

Direct participation was still valued and important in the distribution of wages, but on all the other matters it has in effect been curbed. One noted a growing feeling that management should be given a greater mandate in decision-making. This mandate would be restricted to a given time-period, and could be evaluated annually or biannually, but a greater degree of individual decision-making during those periods should be left to the management team. Still, according to the new Enterprise Law of 1989 and its amendments the enterprises were to have exclusive responsibility for the election of the general managers, thus excluding local authorities, Party institutions, and trade unions (Warner 1990).

Participation was increasingly viewed as something that should also be based on workers' individual expertise, and not exclusively on their rights as employees. The traditional culture of participation and the existing participation channels were envisaged to be used to increase the number and level of innovations.

Poland

The decade 1976–86 was marked in Poland by the continuing fall of the one-party political rule and its economic emanation—central planning. The essential stages of this breakdown in the political scene were: (1) formation, legalization, and continuing rapid expansion of the 'Solidarity' movement in the years 1980–1, (2) martial law in the period 1981–3, and (3) unsuccessful efforts of political reforms within the general framework of the former system.

The early 1980s led to several new developments, such as:

- frequent changes of personnel in the party leadership and in the government;
- formal approval of far-reaching economic reforms;
- the establishment of a pluralistic trade union system followed by the de-legalization of all former trade unions (the Solidarity Movement remained illegal);
- changes in the political power structure with the increased share of small co-ruling parties and with the introduction of political representation to social groups and forces, like the Catholic Church, within the framework of the Consultatory Council, etc.;
- an essential change in political style with much bigger doses of open official and public criticism in all spheres of social life and the creation of some space for open, though formally illegal political opposition.

From the perspective of political change this period can be seen as a predecessor of the final fall of the communist system in Poland. At the same time the Polish economy underwent a series of perturbations including a dramatic fall in the level of national income in the years 1979–82 (around 25 per cent in total) and a continuing rise of the foreign debt.

The most important political and economic factors affecting attitudes towards participation problems were:

- a continuing shortage of labour, especially unskilled;
- inflationary markets which—in a situation of administrative price-control of almost 50 per cent of the total market output, accompanied by central distribution of material and financial resources – caused great deformations in production, consumption, and social attitudes;
- strong political support for the idea of workers' self-management by all the main forces, though for various reasons. This created the impression that a participatory economy was generally accepted as the most desired end of the socio-economic changes.

The events of 1980–1 brought to an end the former system of industrial relations. Growing social criticism undermined the legal structures of the Seventies: the Central Council of Trade Unions at the national level and the 'Conferences of Workers' Self-Managements' and Party Basic Organizations at the enterprise level. Those, Communist Party-dominated participative structures were rejected in the middle of 1981 by the majority of workers. From the end of 1980 till December 1981, when martial law was announced, there developed a pluralistic system of trade unions, dominated by the 'Solidarity' social and political movement.

The Polish Parliament (Sejm) accepted new laws 'On Workers' Self-Management in State Enterprises' and 'On State Enterprises' in September 1981. After a pause caused by the martial law, a process of forming new participative structures continued during the period 1983–7.

By the end of 1983 a vast network of Workers' Councils existed all across the entire Polish industry. The number of elected self-management organs grew by the end of 1986 to 6,400. Thus, 88 per cent of all state-owned enterprises introduced this form of participative structure (defence and partially public sector industries were excluded by the legislators). The number of councils was actually 11, 115, including 5,715 department and factory level councils in large enterprises, with 137, 367 elected members in them, representing formally more than 6 million employees in state industry (Peretiatkowicz 1989).

This impressive participation structure played an essential role in Polish industrial relations in the 1980s. However, field observations provided evidence that the Workers Councils had a limited impact on the actual position of rank-and-file workers and did not always lead to their active participation in most of the enterprises' activities.

According to reliable information in 1986, for example, only about 20 per cent of all elected Workers' Councils played an active role in running their enterprises (Dryll 1987). There is enough evidence to suggest that even most of the active Workers' Councils concentrated their attention mainly on strategic problems, taking little or no interest in the problems related to work organization or current decisions (Gilejko 1987). Some authors even concluded that Self-Management did not reach the department level and that it only strengthened the hierarchical structure of management without leading to any qualitative changes at the workplace level (Grela 1987).

Since 1983 the trade unions—except 'Solidarity', which was forced to continue an illegal activity—were reactivated in most of the enterprises. They started to co-operate with the Workers' Councils as partner organs, and participated in decision-making. Although there is no evidence of any open conflicts between the trade union and the self-management organs, their competencies were not divided clearly enough.

The legal trade union movement was during all the 1983–7 period dominated by the 'All-Poland Agreement', co-operating with the ruling communist party.

Compared with 1977, the industrial relations system in 1981–7 showed indisputable signs of essential changes:

- it allowed for much more space for trade union independence and pluralism;
- there has been an essential rise in the competencies of self-managerial organs in state enterprises;
- the party control over participative organs weakened significantly.

From the point of view of legislation in the field of industrial democracy, the changes in Poland were perhaps more rapid and fundamental than in any other country participating in the IDE project. The laws 'On Workers' Self-Management in State Enterprises' and 'On State Enterprises' of 25 September 1981 increased the legal possibilities of workers' participation in state industry through such procedures as: a general meeting of all workers or their delegates, workers' councils, and referendums. Formal powers of workers' self-management, according to these laws, are quite wide—including a final say in such matters as: profit distribution, long-range production plans, development, modernization, co-determination in appointing managers and their policies, etc.

The second main element of participation structures—trade unions— were modified by the law of October 1982. According to this new law the unions became independent organizations, co-operating with the Workers' Councils and Managements in defending the interests of all employees. The legislators allowed the formation of several trade unions at company level, though in the 1983–7 period this possibility was temporarily halted and the workers could join only the union that was chosen by their majority in the enterprise.

Generally in the years 1981–7 a new legal framework was introduced in Polish state-owned industry. Its idea was to create conditions for the creation of 'self-managed, self-financing and independent' state enterprises. This idea of a 'third way' in the economy was partly reflected by the set of participatory laws. However, it lacked the second of the essential components—changes in economic system. The formally 'independent' enterprises had still to obey the state price-regulating rules, and they were still dependent on governmental decisions concerning levels of taxation, raw materials supplies, wage funds, etc.

In general, during the 1977–87 decade there was insufficient political will and ability to complete the socio-political and economic changes. This was also well reflected in legislation.

The main change in social attitudes towards participation was created by the political events of the years 1980–1. At that time all the main actors of the Polish political scene tried to win social support by advocating the idea of self-management. The governing party reclaimed the decentralization of the economy and the granting to workers the power to run economically independent state enterprises. This was seen as a way of saving the existing political system and the domination of the public sector in the economy. The 'Solidarity' movement united many oppositional parties. Some of them would really accept a 'third way' as an alternative to the centrally planned, party-ruled economic system. The others treated self-management as a tactical target on their strategical way towards destroying the existing system and establishing a privately owned economy.

For the public, and especially for workers, the impression of total support for the idea of self-managed enterprises was overwhelming. All the propositions of reforms which were published in the years 1980–1 were based on Workers' Self-Management (Krawczyk 1981). The level of declared support for participative solutions among the workers became high in 1981 and remained like this until 1987 (Peretiatkowicz 1989). More than 80 per cent of all workers answered in all studies that self-management is 'important' or 'very important' for the management of the enterprises. The centrally planned economy with its high-level social security (full employment, cheap housing, free education and medical care, government price control, etc.) left small room for social initiative in general and at the state enterprises in particular. The workers saw no important reasons for participating actively in any self-managerial or trade union structures. The general attitude in all spheres of social life was not in favour of any form of authentic social activity. People were used to waiting for somebody to solve their problems. This attitude was not essentially changed in the years 1977–87, though growing dissatisfaction led to many protests.

It can be said in conclusion that no social habit of active participation was created in the decade 1977–87 in Poland. For many reasons, it was still much easier to introduce new laws than to create any real form of social activity.

Japan

Joint Consultation System

During the period 1977–87 the Joint Consultation System (Roshikyogi-sei), besides collective bargaining, continued to play a very important role in promoting industrial democracy in Japanese industrial relations. Seventy-one per cent of big companies with over 1,000 employees adopted the system, according to the survey done by the Ministry of Labour in 1982. In that system, representatives of employees at each level of a company—for example, the shop-floor, factory, and company as a whole—meet with their counterparts in management to exchange information about the company's policies, production schedule, changes of shop-floor practices, and so on.

Representatives of employees are usually, in practice, union officials and shop-stewards. Therefore, rigid differentiation between collective bargaining and a joint consultation system is very difficult in the sense that both work effectively to promote communication between management and employees.

About one-third of the labour unions consider that collective bargaining and a joint consultation system cannot be separated for exchanging opinions and for reaching consensus between management and employees. About one-third of the labour unions said that the joint consultation system is a kind of pre-bargaining mechanism which can easily move into collective bargaining when an agreement cannot be reached. Another third of the labour unions insist that a joint consultation system, which usually deals with issues of mutual interest between the management and the employees, can be distinguished from collective bargaining, which usually deals with issues of conflicting economic interests for both parties. The joint consultation system, in any case, presents an effective communication channel for both managers and employees. Having such a channel is the basic condition of industrial democracy.

The joint consultation meetings are usually planned to be held once a month. They are also held as a result of a proposal from both parties or from one of them.

The management at the meeting often give the union representatives confidential information concerning management policies, production plans, financial conditions, introduction of new technology, organizational reform, manning plans, and so on. Union representatives can express their opinions of the management information and give counter-proposals to the management. When the union representatives cannot agree with the management's proposal, the management usually either modifies their proposal in the light of the union's counter-proposal or suspends the execution of the management's proposal for a cooling-off period. The joint consultation system, therefore, does not provide severe conflicts between management and employees.

Some aggressive labour unions criticized the joint consultation system as a mechanism for the management to intensify the employees' involvement in their company and for being only consultation without any power to make decisions. However, the unions Domei, Churitsuroren, and some parts of Sohyo which belong to the private sector took a positive stance towards industrial democracy plans including the joint consultation system as well as collective bargaining. In 1982 45.6 per cent of labour unions researched by the Japan Institute of Labour replied that workers' participation in management is necessary and 29 per cent replied that workers' participation is necessary only for problems relating to working-conditions.

The idea of workers' participation in management, thus, is supported by labour unions, employers, and workers themselves. However, the main practical forms of worker participation in the recent Japanese industrial system are collective bargaining, the joint consultation system, small group activities like quality circles at shop-floor level, and the suggestion system. Employee representation on the board of directors or the co-determination system like the German one will not be accepted at this stage of its development in Japan (for further details see Okubayashi 1989: 67–88).

Conclusions

During the late 1970s and early 1980s, then, we may conclude that the onset of recession was a major shaping factor on how participation evolved. A shift to the political Right was also important, with a less congenial climate for trade unions, who in the tighter economic circumstances were prevailed upon to restrain their demands. The effect on representative participation was uneven as was the impact of structural changes on existing industrial relations systems (see Rojot 1989; Baglioni and Crouch 1990).

In many states, employers' agendas became predominant, but *de facto* involvement varied with labour market strength. Harmonization in the field of workers' participation within the EC advanced very slowly, with less attention being paid to board level than to works' councils, which in some countries like Germany were more clearly defined by the courts. The adoption of new technology also helped move worker involvement further, as higher-skilled employees want more say in decision-making. Generally speaking, however, industrial democracy was on the defensive, if less so in some countries than others. Many managers still kept workers' representatives out of strategic policy-making, even if giving them some say in personnel and operational matters.

3

Comparisons between Countries and over Time

INTRODUCTION

In this chapter we will pay attention to the differences between the countries which participated in the study. The main emphasis will be put on the differences as they appear in the second measurement phase, although some references will be made to the differences with respect to the changes in scores or score patterns over the period 1977–87.

A presentation and discussion of the results of the 1987 cross-national comparisons will be given with respect to (*a*) the formal participative systems (PS), (*b*) the actual involvement practices and distribution of influence in the organizations (PO), and (*c*) the relationships between the two (PS–PO). A separate section will be devoted to each of these three themes.

Formal Norms and Participation

As was described in earlier publications on the subject (IDE 1981*a*), there are three types of norm which regulate or shape the behaviour of members of a social group: folkways, mores, and legal regulations. Folkways are the least explicit and derive their influence primarily from the implicit consensus and acceptance of the members of the group. Mores have a more formalized character in the sense that they are verbally stated and transmitted, and that sanctions are enforced in case individual or social behaviour clearly deviates from the prescribed traditions. Legal norms go even further in that they are written down and enacted as formal rules or legal regulations. Control and enforcing power can be executed on the basis of the law or written-down agreements.

In the IDE study, the last of the three forms of normative regulations (*de jure* participation) is chosen as an independent variable. *De jure* participation, then, refers to the totality of all formal (i.e. written-down), operative rules and regulations that prescribe a certain involvement of various groups in intra-organizational decision-making (IDE 1981*a*). In some countries, there is much more inter-organizational variance then in others. One of the reasons is that in some countries nature and level of the *de jure* participation in organizations are primarily determined by national or industry-wide laws or agreements. In other countries there is more freedom for individual organizations to establish an own-system of rules. Nevertheless it may be interesting to compare the various national patterns in formal participation structure, as they appear in the 1987 data.

In Table 3.1, the total *de jure* participation scores of all groups in the organization are represented. For each group, an average mode score over all sixteen decisions is established, thus describing its overall participative potential, the total *de jure* participation in the organization. The data in Table 3.1 refer to the averages of these company *de jure* participation mode scores for each country for each group.

Looking at the separate scores for the various groups the following conclusions can be made. For the level of workers the formal, *de jure* participation is quite low. With the exception of Yugoslavia, where the score exceeds slightly level 3, all countries score below level 3, which is 'information *ex ante* must be given'. As far as the other countries are concerned, only in Norway, Germany, and Finland does level A score higher then level 2 ('information (unspecified) must be given to the group'). The scores in all other countries are even lower than level 2, the lowest scores being found in Belgium (1.36).

The formal participation power for the level of the first-line supervisor is not much higher than that for the workers' level. Again, with the exception of Yugoslavia all scores fall below level 3, the majority in this case between level 2 and 3. For Belgium, the UK, and the Netherlands the average scores for level B fall below level 2.

As far as the middle-management level is concerned, the data show quite some variety. A low score is found in the UK and the Netherlands, a score between level 2 and 3 in Denmark, Germany, Israel, and Norway. In Sweden, Yugoslavia, Japan, and Poland the score exceeds level 3, and in Finland even level 4 ('obligatory consultation').

In most countries the real formal power is still in the hands of top management. With the exception of the UK, where apparently little formalization and regulation of participative power exist for any level, including top management, most countries display a score for the formal power of top management which exceeds level 3 or even level 4. In Germany, Israel, the Netherlands, Norway, Finland, and Poland the average score is even higher than 5, which indicates that top management must give its approval and, therefore, has veto power over the decision concerned.

The greatest differences are to be found at the level above the company, level E. One finds on the one hand very low formal power (below level 2) in Denmark, Germany, the UK, the Netherlands, Finland, and Poland, while on the other hand, moderate scores (between level 3 and

TABLE 3.1. *Total* de jure *Participation of all Groups in the Whole Organization (1987 data)*

Country	Level	A	B	C	D	E	F	G
Belgium	M[b]	1.36[a]	1.81	2.37	3.67	2.08	2.09	1.09
	S[c]	.37	.83	1.26	1.36	.78	.40	.17
Denmark	M	1.68	2.11	2.50	4.80	1.88	2.45	1.36
	S	.22	.58	.72	.66	.25	.41	.26
Germany	M	2.22	2.14	2.14	5.36	1.27	3.99	1.35
	S	.07	.14	.14	.18	.33	.16	.09
UK	M	1.99	1.69	1.21	1.19	1.19	1.43	1.19
	S	.26	—	.03	—	—	—	—
Israel	M	1.75	2.56	2.50	5.19	3.25	2.69	1.06
	S	—	—	—	—	—	—	—
Netherlands	M	1.89	1.00	1.00	5.38	1.29	3.06	2.31
	S	.16	—	—	—	.03	—	.09
Norway	M	2.72	2.50	2.31	5.90	5.90	3.69	5.11
	S	1.23	.56	—	.16	.6	.56	.17
Sweden	M	1.78	2.57	3.63	4.90	5.68	4.19	1.88
	S	.29	.39	.63	.89	.10	.48	.35
Yugoslavia	M	3.22	3.53	3.76	3.85	—	4.79	1.48
	S	.50	.41	.44	.66	—	.85	.24
Finland	M	2.88	2.36	4.46	5.01	1.59	1.06	1.15
	S	.26	.65	.63	.75	1.00	.16	.32
Japan	M	1.35	2.01	3.39	3.89	3.97	1.63	—
	S	.28	.50	1.22	.79	.89	.59	—
Poland	M	1.67	2.95	3.41	5.47	1.45	3.70	2.27
	S	.19	.21	.54	.54	.57	.32	.47

[a] Average mode of participation scores for groups and countries (total set). Scale from 1–6 (1 = no prescribed involvement, 6 = the group has final say over decision).
[b] Average mode score over organizations.
[c] Variance score over organizations.

4) in Israel and Japan and very high scores (above 5.5) in the Scandinavian countries Norway and Sweden.

It is interesting to analyse the score distribution for level F, the works council or other representative organs within the company. As expected from the nature of the self-management systems which exist in Yugoslavia, in this country the formal power of the works council is the highest (4.7–9) and approaching the level of veto right. On the other hand, in three West European countries (Norway, Sweden, and Germany) and one East European country (Poland) the formal influence is substantial as well (approaching level 4). In countries like the Netherlands and Israel, its score is about 3 (consultative power). For the other countries the formal participative power of the representative body varies from rather moderate to minimal.

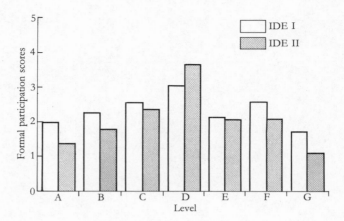

Fig. 3.1 Patterns of Distribution of Formal Power in Organizations, Belgium, 1977–1987

Level G—institutions outside the company, such as national or local government, unions, etc.—generally have a modest formal influence on the decisions made within the company. The exception is Norway where the formal rules seem to give governmental forces an often decisive formal authority over such decision-making. On the basis of some further exploration, it became clear that level G represents a rather mixed category. In certain countries it is clearly reflecting the legally defined rights of national or local governments. In other countries, it reflects more temporary written-down regulation and practices with respect to

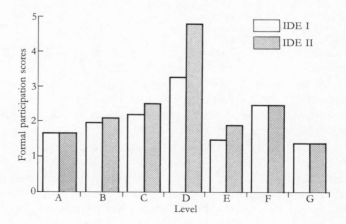

Fig. 3.2 Patterns of Distribution of Formal Power in Organizations, Denmark, 1977–1987

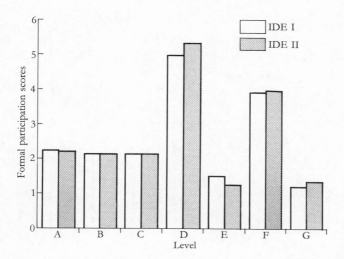

Fig. 3.3 Patterns of Distribution of Formal Power in Organizations, Germany, 1977–1987

influence of banks, unions, supervisory bodies, etc. Moreover, it is not unlikely that idiosyncratic traditions and practices in the particular companies included in the sample also had a strong influence on country-score for G. Conditions such as being an affiliate under the auspices of a big holding company, or being put under control of a bank in view of economic difficulties have determined the particular G-score. It was therefore decided to pay less attention to the G-scores in the further analyses.

In Figures 3.1–3.12, the patterns of distributions of formal power in organizations are depicted. In Figures 3.8*a* and 3.8*b*, two distributions

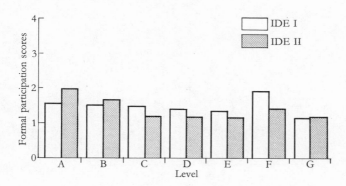

Fig. 3.4 Patterns of Distribution of Formal Power in Organizations, UK, 1977–1987

Comparisons

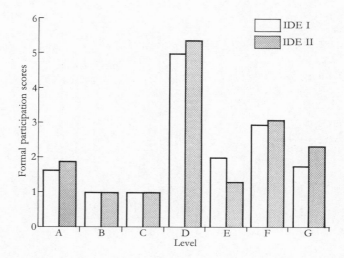

Fig. 3.5 Patterns of Distribution of Formal Power in Organizations, Netherlands, 1977–1987

are given for Sweden. The reason is that in Sweden a replication study was carried out twice: one in 1982 by B. Stymne (Sweden I) and one in 1987 by T. Sandberg (Sweden II). It was judged incorrect to merge the two data-sets into one overall set, in view of both the differences in the distributions in the two re-test studies and the time-lapse of some six years between the two measurements.

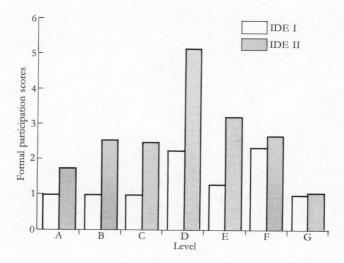

Fig. 3.6 Patterns of Distribution of Formal Power in Organizations, Israel, 1977–1987

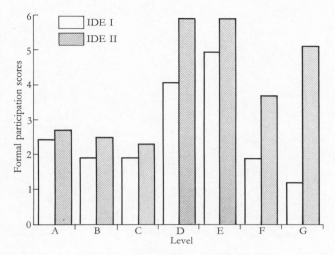

Fig. 3.7 Patterns of Distribution of Formal Power in Organizations, Norway, 1977–1987

As was done in the first publication (IDE 1981*a*: 135), various types of profiles can be distinguished, which are characteristic for the typical patterns of power distribution. In Figures 3.13–3.16 these profiles are presented.

To begin with, there are two unique patterns. First, the 'low-profile patterns', marked by a relatively low score for all groups involved, which was discerned in the UK (Fig. 3.4). In this country, there is little formal regulation of participation, and it is pretty much left to informal

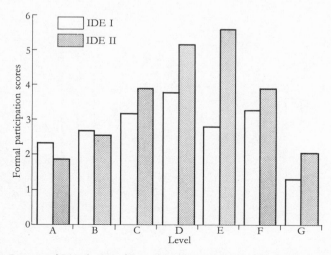

Fig. 3.8a Patterns of Distribution of Formal Power in Organizations, Sweden (I), 1977–1982

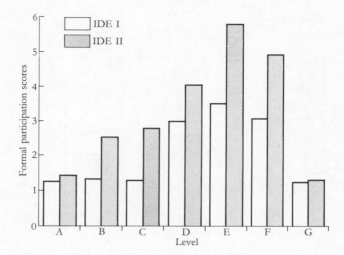

Fig. 3.8b Patterns of Distribution of Formal Power in Organizations, Sweden (II), 1977–1987

developments and interactions. Secondly, there is the representative one-peak pattern characteristic of Yugoslavia. In the latter the highest score is found for the representative organs and the differences in scores between the other groups are rather small. This system calls for a strong formalized control of the decision-making by the workers, although not directly but indirectly through the representative organ.

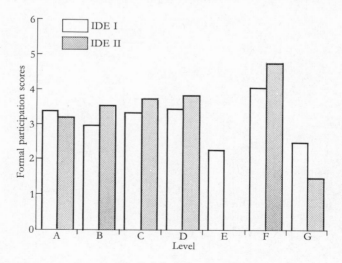

Fig. 3.9 Patterns of Distribution of Formal Power in Organizations, Yugoslavia, 1977–1987

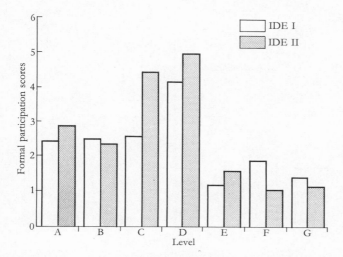

Fig. 3.10 Patterns of Distribution of Formal Power in Organizations, Finland, 1977–1982

Then there are clear 'one-peak patterns', to be found in Belgium (Fig. 3.1), Israel (Fig. 3.6), Norway (Fig. 3.7), and Sweden (Fig. 3.8). The profiles peak in either the top management within the company (top dominance without much control), or the level above the establishment's top management, such as the Supervisory Board or in both (control of top management through or strongly seconded by supervisory bodies). According to the law or formal rules and regulations the power is firmly concentrated in the top or the responsible organ above the top of the companies. This one peak pattern can thus be characterized as hierarchical.

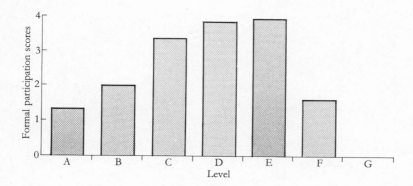

Fig. 3.11 Patterns of Distribution of Formal Power in Organizations, Japan, 1987

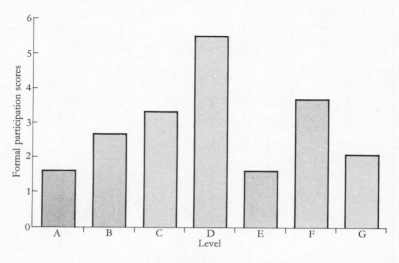

Fig. 3.12 Patterns of Distribution of Formal Power in Organizations, Poland, 1987

In the third place, there is the 'two-peak pattern', to be found in Denmark (Fig. 3.2), Germany (Fig. 3.3), the Netherlands (Fig. 3.5), and Poland (Fig. 3.12). Without exception the highest formal participation score is obtained by the top management (the reason why this pattern can also be named hierarchical), but a moderately high score, indicating the 'second in command' is found for the representative bodies. According to the law and/or formal regulations there should be a reasonable

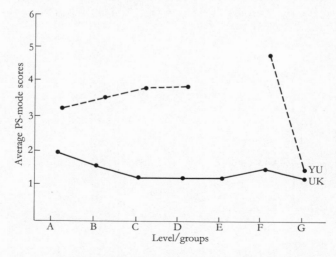

Fig. 3.13 Typical Patterns of Power Distribution

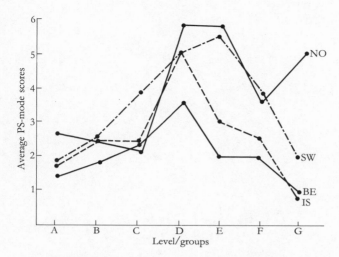

Fig. 3.14 Typical Patterns of Power Distribution

balance of power between these two groups or at least some control of top management through the workers' representation.

Finally there is the 'one-peak pattern', but with a fair sharing of power by middle management. This pattern is found in Finland (Fig. 3.10). The

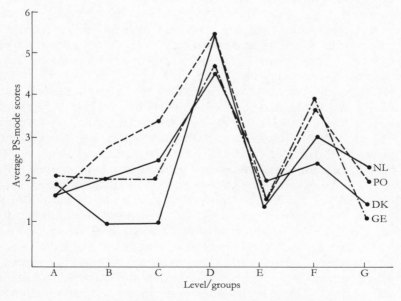

Fig. 3.15 Typical Patterns of Power Distribution

Comparisons

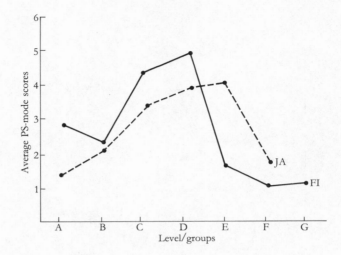

Fig. 3.16 Typical Patterns of Power Distribution

responsibility for a number of decisions (particularly tactical and non-strategic decisions) in Finland is delegated not to the workers' representative organ, nor to a supervisory control organ, but to a rather powerful middle-management. The PS score for the last in Finland was the highest in all the countries under study.

In Japan, too (see also Fig. 3.11), an almost equal balance of formal power between middle and top management is found, but in contrast with Finland the highest formal power in this country is acquired by the supervisory body, whereas the control power for the workers' representation in Japan is very low.

Looking at the variances in standard deviations (see Table 3.1), one is struck by the differences between the countries. This indicates the already-mentioned differences in homogeneity of regulations for formal participation and influence over companies within one given country. In certain countries differences between companies are large, e.g. Belgium, Finland, and Japan. Apparently the formally prescribed power distribution varies strongly over companies. In other countries there is little or hardly any variance (Israel, the Netherlands, Germany). As has been said, this is partly due to the fact that these regulations can be based on national laws, which allow no or only a small deviation for the individual enterprises. Also, other formal regulations can have a strongly general, national character in some countries, whereas in other countries these can be negotiated and coloured by the particular companies.

A comparison of the country profiles for the *de jure* participation distribution with those obtained in the seventies (IDE 1981*a*: 135), shows a

great similarity for a number of countries (see Figs. 3.1–3.12). Great
Britain (Fig. 3.4) has the same low-profile pattern (with a somewhat
higher score for the level of workers in the 1987 data). Yugoslavia (Fig.
3.9) still has the representative one-peak pattern, with even a slight
increase for level F (representative organ). However, it appears that in
1987 in this country the score for workers (A) is somewhat lower, whereas the score for all three supervisory and management levels has increased. Apparently the change in legislation on participation has
caused a (small) shift towards the classical hierarchical power distribution. Of course, in Yugoslavia the workers council remains the organ
with the highest level of *de jure* participative power.

The profile of Belgium (Fig. 3.1) generally is still rather low, but some
differentiation seems to have taken place. A lower score for levels A, B,
C, and F is coupled with a higher score for level D, top management. A
tendency towards the hierarchical one-peak pattern is noticeable.

The profiles for Denmark (Fig. 3.2), Germany (Fig. 3.3), and the Netherlands (Fig. 3.5), all three representatives of the two-peak hierarchical
patterns, have remained almost identical over the past ten years with an
exception of the increase in *de jure* participation for top management
(level D) in Denmark.

In Israel (Fig. 3.6), recent formal company regulations have caused
quite noticeable changes, both in the profile as such, and in the level of
de jure participation in general. With the exception of level F (workers'
council) and G (outside bodies) all levels display a substantial rise in
formal participation, the strongest increase being seen in the supervisory
and management levels and within the board supervisory.

A similar augmentation of formal participative power can be observed
in Norway (Fig. 3.7) and Sweden (Fig. 3.8). Here again, the change in
legislation and formal regulations has affected the absolute *de jure* participative power level of all parties rather than the pattern of distribution
of power over the various levels.

Formal Power-Equalization

The previous analyses have revealed substantial differences between the
countries with respect to the distribution of *de jure* participation over the
various levels in the companies. An interesting indication of the balance
of power between management and workers is the differences in the
scores for formal participation power between management (level D)
and workers (level A). Of course, this is not the only and sometimes not
even a correct indication of formal attempts to 'power equalization'. For
instance, in addition to the workers themselves, a workers' council may
exercise considerable influence, and next to the top management other
supervisory levels within (middle management) or above (supervisory

board) the company can exercise power. Nevertheless, the difference in score level D–A may provide an illustration of the democratization processes in organizations, at least as far as formal prescriptions and legislation are concerned.

In Table 3.2 the difference scores are presented for the short-term, medium-term, and long-term decisions respectively. In the last column the score for the total decision set is presented. Between brackets the rank-order from large (= 1) to small differences (= 12) is given.

Table 3.2 indicates in general a fair amount of difference in formal power over all types of decisions between worker and management levels. The low level of formalization in the UK and the strong democratic control in the legal system in Yugoslavia reveal themselves again. It is striking that the largest differences in formal power between top management and the workers are found in Poland, closely followed by the Netherlands and Israel. Only in the UK., the Netherlands, Yugoslavia, Finland, and Japan is there (some) increase in the differences if one moves from short-term to long-term decisions.

In a number of countries, such as Belgium, Germany, Israel, Sweden, and Poland, the biggest differences are found with respect to the medium-term decisions. In a number of cases this may be due to the influence which the supervisory bodies exercise, which will particularly pertain to the strategic decisions.

In the last column of Table 3.2 the difference-scores for the total set in the first IDE study are presented (IDE 1981*a*: 139). One sees no or only slight differences for the countries Denmark, Germany, Israel, and the Netherlands, a moderate decrease in the UK and Finland, a moderate increase in Sweden and Yugoslavia, and a substantial increase in Bel-

TABLE 3.2. *Top Management–Worker Differences in* de jure *Participation (1987 data)*

Country	Short term	Medium term	Long term	Total	Total IDE I	(Rank)
Belgium	1.93	2.81	2.33	2.30	1.11	(8)
Denmark	3.71	3.06	3.50	3.13	3.01	(5,6,7)
Germany	2.55	4.08	2.14	3.13	3.18	(5,6,7)
UK	− 1.07	− 0.91	0	− 0.18	0.56	(12)
Israel	2.67	4.43	3.00	3.44	3.16	(3)
Netherlands	3.35	3.68	4.00	3.49	3.98	(2)
Norway	3.28	2.92	3.11	3.17	1.65	(4)
Sweden	2.85	3.50	3.03	3.13	2.45	(5,6,7)
Yugoslavia	0.22	0.86	1.28	0.63	− 0.04	(11)
Finland	1.87	2.32	3.20	2.13	2.96	(9)
Japan	1.60	1.84	2.21	1.81		(10)
Poland	3.40	4.21	3.89	3.80		(1)

gium and Norway. It seems that the change in legislation or regulation of participative practices in the latter two countries has led to a relative weakening of the workers' *de jure* influence *vis-à-vis* top management.

A second way of looking at power distribution as far as the prescribed and formalized ways of decision-making is concerned, is to compare the relative influence of top management, levels below top management, and representative body, and to establish the locus of legal decision-making power with respect to different decisions. In Table 3.3 these loci have been symbolized with three different indices: +, v, and 0. These indices signify the following types of power distribution:

+ = Centralized, i.e. average mode score per country is at least 5 (veto power) for top management, or the hierarchical level above top management.

V = Decentralized, i.e. average mode score per country for supervisory and middle management is higher than the average mode score for either top management or the level above.

0 = Democratic, i.e. average mode score per country for the representative body in establishments is at least 4 (consultation is obligatory).

The indices in Table 3.3 in comparison with a similar table based in the first IDE study (IDE 1981*a*: 142 reproduced as Table 3.4) give way to the following conclusions:

- Norway has formal rules and regulations that can be typified as primarily centralized with some democratic predominance. The latter characterization is an addition to the picture in the previous study. Formal rules have democratized and not decentralized the *de jure* participation in Norway.
- Denmark's *de jure* participation system is primarily centralized. For certain types of decisions some room for either decentralization or democratization is created (both stronger than ten years ago), but the primary nature remains centralized.
- For the UK a low level of formalization and little regulation is found, just like ten years ago, and none of the three types applies to the formal UK system.
- In Germany centralization and democratization go hand in hand in the *de jure* participation regulations. All decisions are centralized and almost all decisions democratized, the latter showing even an increase in comparison to the first IDE study.
- The Netherlands shows a *de jure* participation picture almost identical to that of Germany. A very high level of centralization is coupled with a rather high level of democratization. The centralization tendency was extremely high already in the first study, but

TABLE 3.3. *Levels of de jure Decision-making Power for 18 Decisions: Centralized (+), Decentralized (V), Democratized (0) (1987 data)*

Country	Decisions																	
	1	2	3	4	5	6	7	8	9	10	11	12	13	14	15	16	17	18
Norway	0+	+	+	0+	0+	0+	0+	+	0+	+	0+	+	0+	0+	0+		0+	0+
Denmark	0+	+	0+	+	+	+	+		0+	+	+	V		V	V	V	0+	0+
UK									0V	V		V						
Germany	0+	+	0+	0+	0	0+	+	0+	0+	+	0+	+	0+	0+	0+	0+	0+	0+
Netherlands	0+	+	0+	+	0+	0+	0+	+	0+	+	0+	+	+	0+	+	0+	0+	0+
Belgium												V			V	0+		0
Yugoslavia	0V	0	0	0	0V	0	0	0	0	0V	0+	V	0	0V	0	0V	0+	0+
Israel	0+	+	+	0+	+	+	+	+	0+	+V	+	V	0+	0+	0+	0+	+	0+
Sweden	0+	0+	0+		0+	0+	+	0+	0+	+	0+	+	0+	0+	0+	0+	—	—
Finland	+	+	+	V	+	+	+	V	+	V	+	+V	+	+V	+	—		
Japan			+	V	+	+	+		+	V		V	+	V	V		+	+
Poland	0+	+	+	+	+	+	0+	0+	+	V	0+	V	0+		0+	0+	0	0+

V = Mode score of supervisory or middle level > mode score for top managers or level above.
+ = Mode score for top managers, or above > 5.
0 = Mode score for representative bodies > 4.

TABLE 3.4. *Levels of de jure Decision-making Power for 18 Decisions (1977 data)*

Country	Decision															
	1	2	3	4	5	6	7	8	9	10	11	12	13	14	15	16
Norway	+	+	+	+	+	+	+	+	+	+	+	+	+	+	+	+
Denmark	0+	+	0+	+	+		+		+	+	+	V		V	+	+
UK	+												+			
Germany	0+	+	0+	0+	0+	0+	0+	+	0+	+	0+	+	0+	0+	0+	0+
Netherlands	0+	+	0+	+	+	0+	0+	+	0+	+	0+	+	+	0+	+	0+
Belgium	0V		0	0V	0V			0	0	V	0	V	V		0	0
Yugoslavia	0V	0	0	0V					0	0V			0	0	V	0V
Israel	0+	+	+	+	+	+	+		0V	0V	+	+	0+	0	+	0+
Sweden		+	+	V	V	+	+	+	0+	+		V	0+V		+	0
Finland	0+	+	+	+	+	+	+	+			+	+	+	0+		0

the level of democratization has increased somewhat (from 8 out of 16 to 11 out of 18 decisions).
● In Belgium again, the level of formalization of participative power is of such a low level that neither of the three types are applicable.

Formal participation rules in Yugoslavia clearly point to the democratization pattern and even more so than in the IDE I data. In seventeen out of eighteen decisions the Works' Council has at least the right to be consulted. A second but less typical characteristic is decentralization. In six decisions the middle management or supervisory level has more *de jure* power than management.

Israel seems to have a formal system that attributes considerable power to the top levels in the organizations (for seventeen out of eighteen decisions). In addition, a moderate level of democratization is prescribed. Both tendencies, centralization and democratization, seem to be stronger than ten years ago.

Sweden has a pattern almost identical to that of Germany and the Netherlands. Both centralization and democratization are strongly advocated in the legal and formal rules. As compared with ten years ago a remarkable change has occurred. Both centralization and democratization are much stronger now, whereas the tendency to decentralization in the previous study (in a third of the decisions) has almost completely disappeared.

Finland is another country that has undergone substantial changes in the formal participation system. In the first IDE study, the almost sole characteristic was centralization. Only sporadically rules allowed for consultation of the representative body. At present, democratization tendencies are still absent, but middle and lower management have relatively more formal power (decentralization); the main emphasis, however, is still on centralization of decisions.

Japan shows a rather mixed pattern. Although centralization prevails in most decisions there is a fair number of decisions for which the authoritative power, according to the formal regulations, is given to the middle and lower management. In Japan no rules for democratized decision-making, as defined in this study, seem to exist.

In Poland, little delegation is prescribed. The pattern is rather similar to that of Germany, the Netherlands, and Sweden. A strong centralistic tradition and a fair number of decisions in which the representative organ is given right to be consulted.

By way of summary, it can be concluded now that the most frequent pattern is formed by a combination of strong centralization and fairly strong democratization: Norway, Sweden, Germany, the Netherlands, and Poland. A combination of centralization and some decentralization but without democratization is noticed in Finland and Japan. A mainly centralized pattern is found in Israel, and an emphasis on democratization with some room for decentralization in Yugoslavia. The level of formally prescribed participation in two countries (UK and Belgium) is too low to be usable for this typification.

Actual Influence Structure

The empirical research in the IDE study revolved around the main question of how different forms and degrees of formalized rules and regulations for the involvement of employees in organizational decision-making (*de jure* participation) account for the different distributions of actual employee involvement and influence (*de jure* participation). In the previous section of the present chapter, on cross national differences, the variation over countries with respect to the *de jure* participation has been discussed and compared with the IDE I data. In the next section, the same will be done for the *de facto* participation, the actual influence structure.

De facto participation was measured in relation to the groups (levels) and not to individuals. The data in this section are based upon a rating by experts. Key respondents were asked to rate the amount of influence which the different groups/levels have on a five-point scale ranging from 'no influence' (1) to 'very much influence' (5). In Table 3.5 an overview of the average actual influence scores per country for the levels A–G is presented. The following observations can be made on the basis of the data in this table.

TABLE 3.5. *Distribution of Influence, by Country, based on Experts' Judgements (1987 data)*

Country	Level A	B	C	D	E	F	G	All
Belgium	1.75	2.48	3.22	4.00	2.48	2.53	2.01	2.64
Denmark	2.10	2.75	3.09	3.50	1.58	1.63	1.13	2.25
Germany	1.88	2.24	3.41	3.42	1.18	2.69	.099	2.26
UK	2.01	2.70	3.19	3.48	1.98	2.00	1.36	2.40
Israel	1.82	2.65	3.11	4.71	2.71	3.28	2.13	2.92
Netherlands	2.06	2.79	3.20	3.55	1.78	1.95	1.33	2.38
Norway	2.26	2.62	3.40	3.43	1.80	2.22	1.16	2.41
Sweden[a]	2.28	2.78	3.18	3.16	2.63	3.13	1.04	2.60
Yugoslavia	2.44	2.60	3.03	3.64	—	3.44	1.56	2.78
Finland	1.89	2.70	3.78	4.06	1.73	1.43	1.35	2.42
Japan	1.67	2.30	3.07	3.86	3.94	2.19	1.28	2.62
Poland	1.96	3.05	3.72	4.38	1.52	2.95	1.29	2.70
Average	2.01	2.64	3.28	3.77	1.90	2.21	1.39	

[a] Average score for the two sub-samples (I and II)

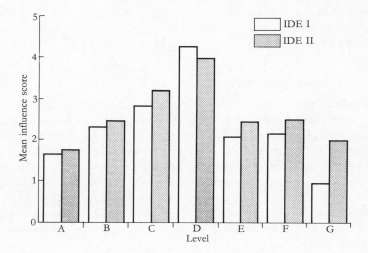

Fig. 3.17 *Influence Distribution, Belgium, 1977–1987*

As in the first study (IDE 1981*a*: 152), it can be concluded that variation across hierarchical levels is much stronger than across countries. The average amount of influence per country varies from 2.25 (Denmark) to 2.92 (Israel), but for levels *within* the company the scores vary from 1.90 (representative organ) and 2.01 (level of workers) to 3.77 (top management). As in the first study, it still appears that the hierarchical ordering is a much stronger determinant of differences in influence than any factor related to the national country characteristics.

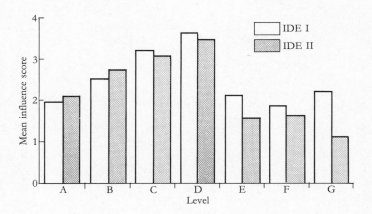

Fig. 3.18 *Influence Distribution, Denmark, 1977–1987*

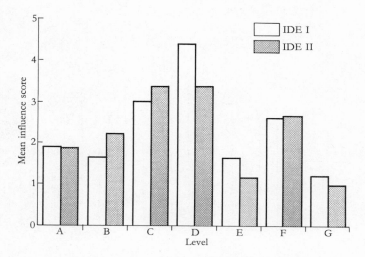

Fig. 3.19 Influence Distribution, Germany, 1977–1987

The rather moderate average scores for the level of workers (A) and representative bodies (F) (scores of 2.01 and 2.21 respectively) indicate that the power distribution is still traditionally hierarchical, the highest level of influence being located at the level of top management and the lowest at the level of the (representatives of the) workers. Yugoslavia is the only exception to the general pattern of workers and their representatives having between little and moderate influence on decisions. In

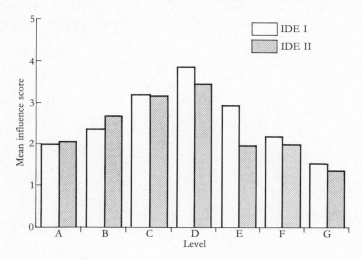

Fig. 3.20 Influence Distribution, UK, 1977–1987

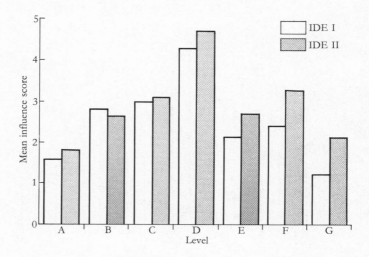

Fig. 3.21 Influence Distribution, Israel, 1977–1987

other words, with an exception of Yugoslavia, the degree of democratization or delegation to the lower levels is still fairly low in all European
countries, but including the Eastern European country Poland and
Japan.

A comparison of the influence distribution within the specific countries to the data from the study ten years ago leads to the following
conclusions (see figs. 3.17–3.26).

The first striking observation is the general similarity between the
mean scores and distributions at the two different points in time. The

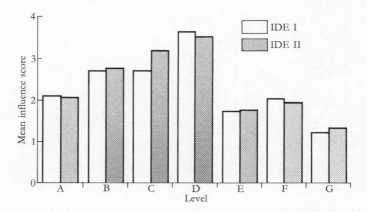

Fig. 3.22 Influence Distribution, Netherlands, 1977–1987

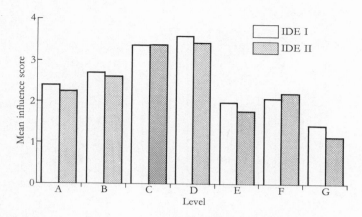

Fig. 3.23 Influence Distribution, Norway, 1977–1987

differences are generally rather small, although sometimes noteworthy at specific levels.

No or hardly any changes in actual influence distribution are found in Finland, the Netherlands, and Norway. A slight (relative) increase in the actual influence level of top management is found in the UK and Yugoslavia. The opposite, a somewhat decreased (relative) powerful position of top management and/or the supervisory body is observed in Belgium, Germany, and Sweden. Hardly any increase in the power position of the workers or workers' council be established (only some changes in Israel and Sweden).

For Japan (Fig. 3.27) and Poland (Fig. 3.28), the two new countries in the 1987 sample, we see a pattern of influence distribution which is quite

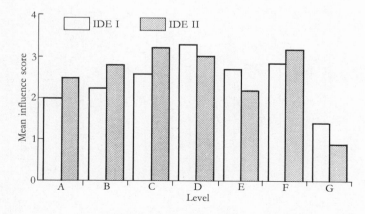

Fig. 3.24a Influence Distribution, Sweden (I), 1977–1982

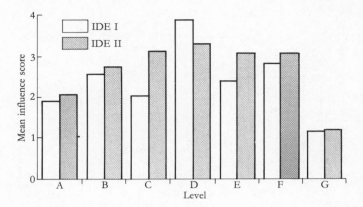

Fig. 3.24b Influence Distribution, Sweden (II), 1977–1987

similar to the patterns of *de jure* participation: in Japan a one-peak hierarchical pattern, with the highest score for the supervisory level above the plant, and in Poland the hierarchical two-peak pattern, with a moderate influence for the workers' representation.

Again it can be said that the actual patterns of power distribution in organizations have remained strikingly similar over the ten-year period, in spite of sometimes significant changes in the political or economic environment. In the conclusion to this chapter we will return to these findings.

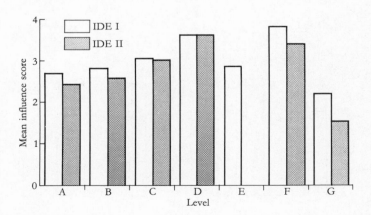

Fig. 3.25 Influence Distribution, Yugoslavia, 1977–1987

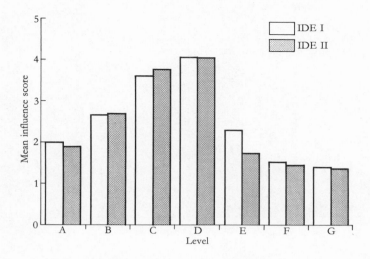

Fig. 3.26 Influence Distribution, Finland, 1977–1982

Relationships between *de jure* and *de facto* Participation

In the final section of this chapter a few cross-national comparisons will be made with respect to the relationship between *de jure* and *de facto* participation for the representative bodies and top management and workers. The findings to be reported here are based solely in the 1987 survey, and the comparisons, therefore, refer to the cross-sectional data, and not to a longitudinal analysis.

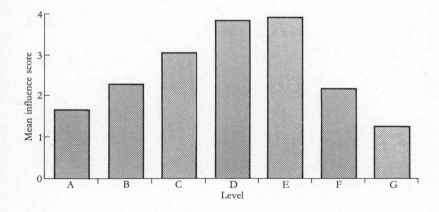

Fig. 3.27 Influence Distribution, Japan, 1987

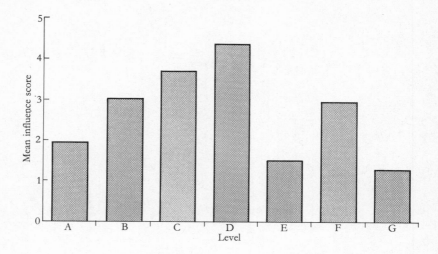

Fig. 3.28 Influence Distribution, Poland, 1987

It should be noted that the scores for the formal participative structure and the actual influence structure as such cannot be compared in an absolute way, since they represent different scale positions and different ranges. The scores on the Formal Participation scale run from 1 (no information) to 6 (complete delegation) and the scores on the Influence

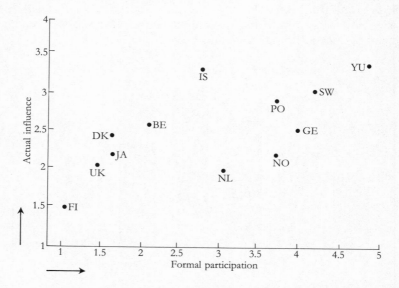

Fig. 3.29 Formal Participation and Influence of Representative Bodies

scale from 1 (no influence) to 5 (very much influence). The comparison, therefore, should be made only in a relative way, so as to indicate the different ranking positions of the countries on both scales.

In Figure 3.29 the various positions of the country-scores for representative bodies in the Formal Participation–Influence matrix are indicated. In general we see a reasonably strong relationship between the two variables. A group of countries (Finland, UK, Japan, Denmark, and Belgium) show a relatively low to moderate score for both the formal participation and the influence dimension. In other countries (Poland, Sweden, and Yugoslavia) both *de jure* and *de facto* participation are relatively strong (although, with the exception of Yugoslavia, still moderate in an absolute sense).

In four countries the combination of scores deviates from the co-variance pattern. In Israel there seems to be a relatively more actual influence of the representative bodies than is indicated by the formal regulations for their participation. In the Netherlands, Norway, and Germany the situation is reversed. The score for formal participation seems to be relatively higher than the score for actual influence, indicating a possible under-utilization of the room for power and influence provided by legal and formal conditions.

A second analysis is presented in Fig. 3.30, in which the patterns of relationships between differences in formal participation and actual influence between levels D and A (top management and workers) are

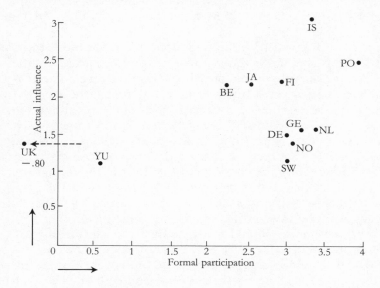

Fig. 3.30 Differences in Formal Participation and Actual Influence between Top Management (Level D) and Workers (Level A), Total Score

represented. It can be seen that in one group of countries, (Sweden, Norway, Denmark, Germany and the Netherlands) the formal and legal regulations allow for more differences in influence between the highest and lowest level in the company than the differences in actual influence reflect. Exactly the opposite is true in Great Britain and Yugoslavia. In the last two countries the (moderate) differences in actual influence between the two levels exceed those for the formal and legal regulations, which indicate hardly any difference in influence. In the other countries, Belgium, Japan, and particularly Poland and Israel a fair amount of difference in influence and power between the highest and lowest levels in the company can be discerned both in legal provisions and norms and in actual practice.

CONCLUSION

In this chapter, the various similarities and differences between the countries in the sample have been examined with respect to the two main variables in the IDE research, the formal participative structure, and the actual influence structure within companies. It was expected that a number of changes in the socio-political and economic context which has taken place during the interval between the two measurements points 1977 and 1987 would have affected both the formal participation and the actual influence distribution; the latter either directly or indirectly through the assumed and in the previous study empirically confirmed causal relationship between the formally prescribed and actual levels of influence.

One of the more striking findings from this replication study, as reported in this chapter, is the fact that the more substantial differences were found primarily in the formal participative area and not as far as the actual influence structure is concerned. In fact, the scores with respect to the latter showed a remarkable stability over the ten years between the two moments of data collection. The inference which forces itself on us is that changes in the socio-political environment may lead to changes in legislation or formal regulations with respect to participation and power in organizations, but that neither the former precondition, nor the latter consequences have a necessary bearing upon the actual influence distribution in enterprises, particularly since this distribution was and is in most cases classic hierarchical.

Before, however, we should adhere to such a conclusion, more detailed analyses are needed. It can be that differences do occur, but are being levelled out in the averaging processes. Moreover, changes in actual influence patterns could need more time and certain change—tendencies which were found (e.g. with respect to top-management level) could be the prelude to actual changes, in time. It can also be that certain changes pertain to particular decisions or types of decisions which do not show themselves in the 'total score' which was mostly used in the comparisons in this chapter.

Therefore a more detailed analysis in which various subgroups, categories of companies, types of decisions, or phases in decision-making are distinguished, seems necessary. Chapter 4 will deal with such a more detailed analysis and its results.

4

Factors Affecting Patterns of Influence Distribution in Organizations

INTRODUCTION

Previous chapters have indicated how patterns of *de jure* participation (PS) and the distribution of influence (PO) in organizations have changed between 1977 and 1987. In this chapter we turn to the relationship between these two central variables (PS and PO).[1] Though in detail the findings of the IDE I study, in this respect, were rather complex (see IDE 1981*b*: chs. 7 & 10) two salient ones stand out. First, institutional norms regulating patterns of participation in decision-making, though by no means explaining all the variance in patterns of influence in organizations, were found to have a more significant effect on the distribution of influence than any of the other independent variables examined, including a series of 'contextual' sociological, technological, structural, and economic factors. The impact of institutional norms on patterns of influence was found to be particularly significant in respect of workers and representative bodies at plant level—the more highly developed the formal rules and regulations for the participation of these two groups in organizational decision-making, the greater the influence of labour over organizational decisions. Second, contextual variables, including structural characteristics of the enterprise, such as technology, size, and sector, were found to be relatively weak additional determinants of the distribution of influence in organizations. Of the contextual variables examined, the one which was found to have the strongest impact on the distribution of influence was the degree of employee mobilization, measured in terms of workers' membership of trade unions and representative bodies at the plant. This variable, which is an index of the organizational strength of labour within the enterprise, was

---

[1] Here the terms '*de jure* participation', 'institutional norms', and 'formal participatory rules' will be used interchangeably to refer to PS; i.e. to the set of formal rules and regulations based on legislation, collective bargaining agreements, and/or management policy, which govern and prescribe the mode or degree of participation of different groups in organisational decision-making.

found to be positively related to the influence of both workers and their representatives at the plant. It was also found to be associated with a generally more equal distribution of influence between management and labour within the enterprise.

The aim of this chapter is to explore the extent to which patterns of influence distribution are conditioned by the institutional framework for participation and by contextual factors, using the 1977 and 1987 data sets as the basis for our analysis. In order to do this we first present a re-analysis of the 1977 data using institutional norms and selected contextual variables as co-predictors of patterns of influence. Using the same set of variables and procedures we then look at the data from the 1987 replication study and compare the results of this analysis with those for the 1977 data. In the second part of the chapter we look at the IDE data from a longitudinal perspective and examine the relationship between changes in the distribution of influence and changes in the institutional framework for participation and in contextual factors between 1977 and 1987. In the process, we examine a number of alternative explanatory models of influence and, on the basis of this analysis, provide an overall interpretation of observed changes in patterns of influence distribution between 1977 and 1987.

CROSS-SECTIONAL ANALYSIS

The Pattern in 1977: A Recomputation

Methodological Issues

We start by recomputing a model for some of the IDE I, 1977 data. This has been done for three reasons. First, since the 1987 data contain no cases from France and Italy a reduced data set for 1977 was used, dropping the firms from these two countries from the original data set. This more readily facilitates comparison of patterns in 1977 and 1987. Second, in 1987, because of the more limited resources at our disposal, we were unable to collect data on as wide a range of contextual variables as in 1977. We were also unable to obtain reliable figures on trade union membership across the full sample of organizations. In order to facilitate comparisons of patterns in 1977 and 1987, therefore, a new set of regressions were computed for 1977, using as regressors only those contextual variables for which data were available also for 1987.

Finally, in order to examine the impact of the business cycle and of the general state of the labour-market on the distribution of influence in 1977 and 1987, two new macro-economic variables were added to our data. These two variables are the average annual percentage growth in GDP between 1975 and 1977 and between 1985 and 1987 respectively, and the annual average percentage rate of unemployment per country over the same two three-year periods. Preliminary analysis of the data showed these two sets of variables to be highly negatively intercorrelated across the ten countries in both time-periods. The unemployment rate, however, was found to be more strongly correlated with various dimensions of the distribution of influence than was the rate of growth in GDP. The GDP variable was therefore dropped from the analysis in favour of the unemployment rate, which was retained as a co-predictor of influence and used in the subsequent multivariate analyses carried out on both the 1977 and 1987 data.

The main dependent and independent variables used in the new analysis of the 1977 data to be presented in this chapter, including the new unemployment variable, are listed in Figure 4.1. (For a discussion of how each of the variables was measured and constructed see Chapter 3 and

Independent Variables

Institutional (PS) Variables

De jure Participation (PS) score per level
Workers (Level A)
Supervisors (Level B)
Middle Manangement (Level C)
Top Management (Level D)
Representative Bodies (Level F)
Relative *de jure* Participation (PS) Scores
Management-Workers (M-W)
Management-Representative Bodies (M-R)

Dependent Variables

Influence(PO) Variables

Influence (PO) score per level
Workers (Level A)
Supervisiors (Level B)
Middle Management (Level C)
Top Management (Level D)
Representative Bodies (Level F)
Relative Influence (PO) Scores
Management-Workers (M-W)
Management-Representative Bodies (M-R)

Contextual Factors

1. Macro-economic Variables
    Average Unemployment Rate (1975–7)
    Average Unemployment Rate (1985–7)

2. Organization-Specific Contextual Variables
        Size of Organization
        Formal Independence
        Sector (Manufacture/Service)
        Functional Differentiation
        Vertical Span (No. hierarchical levels)
        Degree of Formalization
        Level of Automation
        Skill-Level Requirements
        Percentage Skilled Workers
        Work-flow Interdependance
        Product Complexity
        Perceived Market Dominance
        Perceived Political Instability

Fig. 4.1 Dependent and Independent Variables Used in the Multivariate Analysis of the 1977 and 1987 IDE Data

Appendix A) Note that the independent variables used in the analysis include two main types of contextual factors: (i) the unemployment rate, which is a macro-economic variable measured at a country level, and (ii) organization-specific contextual variables which include primarily structural and technological characteristics of the enterprise and are measured at the level of the organization. In the following analysis the unemployment rate will be treated separately from the other 'contextual variables' listed in Figure 4.1. For the sake of clarity, therefore, the unemployment rate will, hereafter, be referred to simply as an 'economic' variable, while the term 'contextual variables' will be used exclusively to refer to the set of organization-specific contextual variables listed under this heading in Figure 4.1.

Note also that in this chapter we will not look at all the different groups identified in the research (levels A–G), or present a detailed analysis of the data broken down by individual clusters of decisions. In order to simplify both the presentation and discussion of results, we will restrict our analysis to the five main internal organizational groups covered in the study, i.e. workers, first-line supervisors, middle and top management, and representative bodies at the plant (levels A, B, C, D, and F), and focus primarily on patterns of influence distribution over the total set of sixteen decisions. The 1977 and 1987 results for specific clusters of decisions are reported in full in Appendix A but will not be discussed in detail in the body of the chapter.[2] As part of the analysis, however, we will also examine key aspects of the distribution of influence between management and labour in organizations. In order to do this, two new measures of relative influence were constructed for use as dependent variables in the analysis: (*a*) the relative influence of management and workers, and (*b*) the relative influence of management and representative bodies at the plant (see Fig. 4.1). These measures are designed to assess the extent of equalization of influence between management and labour in organizations. They were constructed by first combining (averaging) the influence scores of all three management groups (i.e. supervisors, middle management and top management) over the total decision set, and then subtracting from this score the influence score for workers and for representative bodies respectively— the higher the resulting score the greater the influence of management compared to that of workers and/or their representatives over the set of sixteen decisions. Parallel sets of measures were also constructed for *de jure* participation for use as independent variables in the relevant 1977 and 1987 regression analyses (see Fig. 4.1).

---

[2] The results of both the 1977 and 1987 analyses for external groups (level G) and for level E, the level above the enterprise, which includes supervisory boards and corporate management, are available from the IDE International Research Group upon request.

TABLE 4.1. *Re-analysis of 1977 Data: Regressions of Influence (PO 1977) on to other Variables (1977) for the Total Decision Set, by Level*

Predictors (1977 values)	Regression Equations (A to M-R)						
	A Influence workers	B Influence supervisors	C Influence middle management	D Influence top management	F Influence representative bodies	M-W Influence management-workers	M-R Influence management-representatives
PS score per level (A to M-R)	0.29*	–	+	–	0.64	0.31	0.42
Unemployment rate	0.27	0.30	–	+	0.22	–	–0.24
Market dominance	+		–	–0.25		–0.19	–
Political instability					+		+
Sector	+		+				
Product complexity	+			0.36			
Functional difference					+		
Formalization		–0.31		–0.39		–0.19	–0.25
Adjusted R²	0.28	0.11	0.03	0.21	0.59	0.27	0.44
(N)	(88)	(87)	(81)	(88)	(82)	(88)	(86)

Key:

Influence (PO) Measures used as Dependent Variables in Regression Equations A to M-R

Equations A, B, C, D and F: Mean influence (PO) score of levels A, B, C, D and F respectively over set of 16 decisions.

Equation M-W: Mean influence (PO) score of three management groups over 16 decisions minus mean influence (PO) score of workers over 16 decisions.

Equation M-R: Mean influence (PO) score of three management groups over 16 decisions minus mean influence (PO) score of representative bodies over 16 decisions.

De Jure Participation (PS) Measures used as Predictors of Influence in Equations A to M-R

Equations A, B, C, D and F: Mean *de jure* participation (PS) score of levels A, B, C, D and F respectively over set of 16 decisions.

Equation M-W: Mean *de jure* participation (PS) score of three management groups over 16 decisions minus mean *de jure* participation (PS) score of workers over 16 decisions.

Equation M-R: Mean *de jure* participation (PS) score of three management groups over 16 decisions minus mean *de jure* participation (PS) score of representative bodies over 16 decisions.

* Numbers in the table are standardized regression coefficients.

Initial Recomputation

The new analysis of the 1977 data is summarized in Table 4.1. The table shows the results of a linear additive regression of measures of influence for each level, over the total decision set, on to a series of predictor variables, including measure of *de jure* participation for each level. The regressions are reported columnwise for each level (A–F) and for the two selected relative influence scores designed to measure key aspects of the distribution of influence between management and labour in organizations.

Since the number of observations is not large the following estimation procedure was employed. First, the influence score for each level was regressed on to the full set of organization-specific contextual predictor variables listed in Figure 4.1. Those variables gaining 5 per cent significance were then introduced into a second set of regressions of influence for each level, using also the unemployment rate and the corresponding formal participation scores for each level as predictor variables. Numerical values of those standardized coefficients gaining significance, at least the 5 per cent level, are reported in the table, along with the signs (+ or −) of those other variables introduced but which failed to gain significance.

Inspection of Table 4.1 seems, by and large, to reconfirm our earlier (1977) findings concerning the salience of *de jure* participation as a predictor of the influence of both workers and representative bodies at the plant. More specifically, the re-analysis of the 1977 data suggests that the influence of these two groups is enhanced by the existence of formal rules and regulations which promote and legitimize their participation in organizational decision-making. The impact of facilitating norms of this kind is particularly strong in the case of representative bodies. Institutional norms do not appear to have a significant impact on the influence of any of the three main management levels within the enterprise (i.e. top and middle management and first-line supervisors). The institutional framework of participation does, however, hold up as a reasonable predictor of the relative influence of managerial groups in relation to both workers (M-W) and their representatives (M-R).

In so far as the contextual variables are concerned, the results, in general, suggest that they tend to be relatively weak predictors of patterns of influence in organizations, thereby reconfirming the findings of our earlier study. As can be seen from Table 4.1, none of the contextual variables has a significant effect on the overall influence of either workers or representative bodies. With the exception of top management (level D), contextual variables also appear to have little impact upon the influence of management groups within the enterprise. For top management, 'product complexity' seems to increase their influence and 'market dominance' and 'formalization' to reduce it, with formalization

TABLE 4.2. *Re-analysis of 1977 Data excluding Yugoslavia: Regressions of Influence (PO 1977) on to other Variables (1977) for the Total Decision Set, by Level*

Predictors (1977 values)	Regression Equations (A to M-R)						
	A Influence workers	B Influence supervisors	C Influence middle management	D Influence top management	F Influence representative bodies	M-W Influence management-workers	M-R Influence management-representatives
PS score per level (A to M-R)	–	–	+	–	0.64	0.25	0.25
Unemployment rate	–0.30*	–	+	0.32	–0.24	0.37	0.36
Market dominance	+		–	–0.20		–	–
Political instability					+		+
Sector	0.31		+				
Product complexity	+			0.41			
Functional difference					+		
Formalization		–0.32		–0.31		–	–0.24
Adjusted R^2	0.16	0.10	0.02	0.30	0.40	0.26	0.40
(N)	(80)	(78)	(73)	(80)	(74)	(80)	(78)

Key: As in Table 4.1.

* Numbers in table are standardized regression coefficients.

having a marginally stronger effect. Formalization, which is usually seen as an indicator of bureaucratization, also reduces the influence of supervisors over the total decision set and is the only contextual variable which appears to have a significant effect on the overall distribution of influence between management and labour. Formalization does not have a direct impact on the influence of workers and representative bodies. Because of its negative effect on management groups, however, it tends to be associated with a more equal distribution of influence within the enterprise (M-W and M-R). More generally, our results lend support to the idea that formalization tends to limit the discretionary power of management and can therefore work to the advantage of subordinate groups and contribute to a greater equalization of influence in organizations (Gouldner 1954; Crozier 1964; Mintzberg 1983).

Turning now to the unemployment variable, Table 4.1 suggests that the state of the labour-market has a significant effect on patterns of influence in organizations. In line with much of the literature on industrial relations, we expected the unemployment rate to be positively related to the influence of management and negatively related to that of labour (Batstone 1988; Kelly and Richardson 1989; Kochan, Kate, and McKersie 1986; Ramsey 1983). Surprisingly, however, unemployment appears to have a positive rather than a negative impact on the influence of both workers and representative bodies. This suggests some kind of counter-cyclical effect with high unemployment enhancing rather than reducing the influence of labour in organizations.

A closer examination of the data suggests, however, that these results may simply be a function of country-specific effects and, in particular, of the fact that in Yugoslavia in 1977 high levels of labour influence happened to coincide with high levels of unemployment. As noted in the previous chapter, Yugoslav firms had by far the highest influence scores for workers and representative bodies in 1977. At the same time the unemployment rate in Yugoslavia was also much higher than in any other country—9.1 per cent as compared to an average of 2.8 per cent for the remaining countries in the sample. These extreme values for Yugoslavia could, in turn, help to account for the positive relationship found between the rate of unemployment and the level of influence of workers and their representatives over the 1977 sample as a whole. In order to check for this possibility the regressions in Table 4.1 were recomputed without the Yugoslav firms. The results of this new analysis are reported in Table 4.2.

Final Recomputation

As can be seen from Table 4.2, dropping the Yugoslav cases from the analysis substantially changes some of the results for the 1977 data. Three main points stand out in this respect. First, the exclusion of Yugoslavia tends to weaken the overall predictive power of our regression models, except in the case of top management (level D) (see the adjusted R^2 figures at the bottom of Tables 4.1 and 4.2 respectively). Second, while the exclusion of Yugoslavia does not seem to affect the pattern of results for the contextual variables it significantly changes the picture with respect to the unemployment variable. In particular, inspection of Table 4.2 shows that the coefficients for the unemployment variable are now in the expected direction—increasing unemployment enhances the influence of top management and reduces that of workers and their representatives at the plant. The unemployment rate also emerges as a stronger predictor of the relative influence of management and labour within the enterprise than was suggested by the previous analysis (Table 4.1), with high unemployment tending, as expected, to be associated with a less equal distribution of influence between management and labour (M-W and M-R in Table 4.2).

Finally, comparison of Tables 4.1 and 4.2 shows that the exclusion of Yugoslavia from the analysis tends to weaken the effect of PS as predictors of patterns of influence in organizations, particularly in the case of workers (level A). For this level, the PS variable is no longer a significant predictor of influence once the Yugoslav firms are excluded from the analysis. As noted in the previous chapter, these are the firms which had by far the highest levels of *de jure* participation for both workers and representative bodies in 1977, reflecting Yugoslavia's more highly developed formal framework for participation in the 1970s as embodied and institutionalized in its system of self-management. The fact that the coefficient for the PS variable fails to reach significance once the cases with the highest scores on this variable are excluded from the analysis, suggests that the relationship between *de jure* participation and influence may be more complex than was indicated in our earlier study (IDE 1981*a*; 1981*b*). In particular, it suggests that the relationship between these two central variables may be non-linear with institutional norms having a noticeable effect on the influence of workers and, possibly also of representative bodies, only when they sanction a certain level of participation for labour (e.g. the right to have a say or to be consulted before a decision is taken rather than just to be informed about the decision). Below this level formal participatory rules may not significantly help to enhance the influence of labour.

In order to test this possibility the PO scores for workers and for representative bodies were regressed on to the appropriate PS scores for each of these two groups. This bivariate procedure was then repeated using first a log and then a squared transformation of the PS variable as a regressor. The results of this analysis do not lend much support to the non-linear hypothesis.[3] Using the log or the squared transformations

---

[3] Results available from the IDE Group upon request.

does not appear significantly to improve the predictive power of the regression equations. Clearly, the possibility of some kind of non-linear relationship cannot be ruled out completely since some other type of transformation could prove to fit the data better. Given the present results, however, in the remainder of this chapter we will continue to use the absolute value of PS as a predictor of PO.

Summary of Results for 1977

In summary, our re-analysis of the 1977 data tends, by and large, to reconfirm the findings of the earlier IDE I study. In particular, it reconfirms the importance of institutional norms (PS) as predictors of the influence of representative bodies at the plant as well as of the overall distribution of influence between management and labour in organizations. It also reconfirms the fact that contextual variables, with some exceptions, tend to be relatively weak additional predictors of influence in organizations, especially in respect of workers and representative bodies. (See also the results of the more detailed analysis of the 1977 data by specific clusters of decisions reported in Appendix A, Tables A1–A3.)[4]

Our re-analysis of the 1977 data also suggests, however, that the relationship between *de jure* participation and patterns of influence may be more complex than was assumed in IDE 1981*b*. In particular, it suggests that institutional norms may have a more limited impact on worker influence than was indicated in our earlier study, possibly reflecting some kind of threshold effect of *de jure* participation with formal rules helping to enhance worker influence only if they sanction a certain level of participation for this group. For workers, the general state of the labour-market appears to be a better predictor of influence than is the institutional framework of participation—the higher the unemployment rate the lower is the influence which workers have over organizational decisions. Sector also seems to have some effect, with workers in service-sector organizations tending to have more influence than their counterparts in manufacturing industry. For workers, however, the overall predictive power of our mixed model combining institutional norms, the rate of unemployment, and contextual variables is limited, accounting for only 16 per cent of the variance in the influence of this group over the total set of decisions.

The model works much better for representative bodies and for top management accounting for 40 and 30 per cent of the variance respect-

[4] Note that in all cases Yugoslavia was excluded from this more detailed analysis of the 1977 data since the unemployment rate was used as one of the main co-predictors of patterns of influence over individual clusters of decisions. The results in Tables A1, A2, and A3 should, therefore, be compared to those for the total decision set-up in Table 4.2 which also exclude Yugoslavia. The results for 1977 by decision cluster but including Yugoslavia are available from the IDE Group upon request.

TABLE 4.3. *Analysis of 1987 Data: Regressions of Influence (PO 1987) on to other Variables (1987) for the Total Decision Set, by Level*

Predictors (1987 values)	Regression Equations (A to M-R)						
	A Influence workers	B Influence supervisors	C Influence middle management	D Influence top management	F Influence representative bodies	M-W Influence management-workers	M-R Influence management-representatives
PS score per level (A to M-R)	0.50			+	0.60	0.25	0.44
Unemployment rate	–	–	–	0.32	+	+	+
Formal independence	+	–	+				
Skill requirements		–					
Product complexity	+		+		+		–0.33
Functional difference	+		+				
Adjusted R^2	0.25	0.03	0	0.07	0.41	0.09	0.29
(N)	(66)	(65)	(64)	(66)	(51)	(66)	(61)

Key: As in Table 4.1.

* Numbers in table are standardized regression coefficients.

ively in the influence of these two groups over the total decision set. The overall influence of representatives bodies at the plant is affected by two main factors. In order of their importance these are (i) institutional norms which promote and legitimate representatives' participation in organizational decision-making, and (ii) the rate of unemployment which, as expected, has a negative impact on their overall influence over organizational decisions.

The unemployment rate emerges as an important predictor also of the influence of top management, although for this group the impact, as expected, is in a positive direction. Apart from the unemployment rate, the influence of top management, like that of other management groups within the enterprise, is predicted mainly by contextual variables, including product complexity, market dominance, and structural characteristics of the enterprise, such as the degree of formalization of the organization. It should be noted, however, that for supervisors and middle management (levels B and C) the effect of contextual variables, although significant, is not very marked. For these two groups the overall explanatory power of our model is very limited.

Finally, turning to the measures of relative influence, our reanalysis of the 1977 data suggests that the distribution of influence between management and labour is mainly a function of three factors: the institutional framework of participation (PS), the unemployment rate, and the degree of formalization or bureaucratization of the organization. More specifically, institutional norms which promote the participation of workers and their representatives in organizational decision-making while limiting that of management groups within the enterprise, tend to contribute to a more equal distribution of influence between management and labour in organizations. Similarly, a tight labour-market and an emphasis on the formalization of organizational rules and procedures also tend to contribute to a greater equalization of influence between management and labour.

The Pattern in 1986: Differences and Similarities with 1976

Methodological Considerations

We turn now to an examination of the 1986 data using the same procedures and estimation techniques used for the 1976 data. The results of this analysis for the total decision set are shown in Table 4.3. The 1986 results for specific clusters are presented in Tables A4–A6 in Appendix A. Note that in all cases the Yugoslav firms are included in the analysis even though for 1986, like for 1976, the unemployment rate is being used as one of the main co-predictors of patterns of influence, along with institutional norms and a selected number of contextual variables. The main reason for including the Yugoslav cases in the 1986 analysis is that between 1976 and 1986 unemployment rates in Yugoslavia rose less sharply than in most of the other countries in our study. Compared to 1976, therefore, Yugoslavia's unemployment rate in 1986 is more in line with that of other countries thereby making it unnecessary to exclude the Yugoslav firms from the 1986 analysis as was done for the 1977 data.[5]

Comparison of patterns in 1977 and 1987 is, however, complicated by the fact that in 1987 it was not possible to collect data on key contextual variables for a number of organizations in our sample. For 1987, therefore, our full 'institutional–economic–contextual' model can only be tested on a more limited subset of organizations even though data on both the PS and the unemployment variables are available for the sample as a whole. The number of organizations which drop out of the 1987 analysis because of missing data on the contextual variables varies depending on the particular regression equations involved. In some instances, though, up to 30 per cent of the cases in the sample drop out of the analysis (see bottom line in Table 4.3). Moreover, the majority of these cases come from just two countries, Finland and Sweden, indicating that the missing cases are not randomly distributed across our sample. Before we can compare patterns in 1977 and 1987, therefore, we first need to check the robustness of the 1987 results and see whether the missing cases make a significant difference to the analysis. This involves testing our model, without the contextual variables, on (*a*) the full 1987 sample, and (*b*) the subset of organizations for which data are available on the contextual variables, and then comparing the regression coefficients for the PS and the unemployment variables from these analyses with those in Table 4.3. The more stable the coefficients, the more robust can the 1987 results be said to be. In turn, the more robust are the results, the more confident we can be that any differences between the data in Table 4.3 and the corresponding results for 1977 (Table 4.2) reflect 'real' differences in patterns between the two time-periods rather than just being a function of the more limited subset the organizations used in the 1987 analysis.

The specific procedures used to check the robusters of the 1987 results are reported in full in Appendix B, along with the detailed results of the tests which were carried out on the 1987 data for levels A, B, C, D, and F and for the two relative influence measures (M-W and M-R). Two main

---

[5] From 1985 to 1987 the unemployment rate in Yugoslavia reached 13%, compared to 18% and 16% in Belgium and Holland respectively, and between 9% and 11% in countries like Germany, Denmark, and the UK. The exclusion of Yugoslavia from the analysis does not, in any case, significantly affect the overall regression results for 1987, thereby further justifying using the full data set for the 1987 analysis. (The results of the 1987 analysis for the total decision set and by decision cluster, excluding Yugoslavia, are available from the IDE Group upon request.)

points emerge from this analysis. Firstly, the 1987 results relating to the PS variable tend, on the whole, to be reasonably robust. Thus, only one out of the seven PS coefficients examined (for levels A, B, C, D, and F and for M-W and M-R) shows any signs of instability; i.e. changes significantly depending on whether the analysis is carried out on the full 1987 sample or only on the more limited subset of organizations for which data on the contextual variables are also available. The coefficient in question is that for the distribution of influence between management and workers (M-W). The second point to note is that the results relating to the unemployment variable tend, by and large, to be less robust then those for the PS variables. Three out of the seven unemployment coefficients examined show signs of instability, including the coefficient for workers (level A) and those for the relative influence measures. In all these cases the predictive power of the unemployment variable tends to vary significantly depending on the organizations and/or variables included in the analysis. In brief, the tests carried out on the 1987 data suggest that some of the regression results in Table 4.3 do not necessarily hold for the sample as a whole and, consequently, need to be interpreted with caution, particularly when they are being used for comparisons with the 1977 data.

Impact of Institutional Norms

Comparison of Table 4.3 with the corresponding table for 1977 (Table 4.2) shows that there are important similarities as well as differences between the 1977 and 1987 results. The greatest similarities are to be found in respect of the impact of institutional norms on patterns of influence in the two time-periods. In the main the PS results for 1977 reappear in 1987. In particular, in 1987 the institutional framework for participation emerges once again as a key predictor of the influence of representative bodies over organizational decisions. The impact of the institutional framework on labour appears, if anything, to be more pronounced in 1987 than in 1977. Thus, as Table 4.3 shows, for 1987 institutional norms are the best (and only) predictors not just of the influence of representative bodies over the total decision set, but also of that of workers.

Closer examination of the data shows, however, that the regression results for workers are significantly affected by the presence within the 1987 sample of a small number of outlying cases with unusually high scores on the PS variable. Two organizations in particular stand out in this respect, each with an average *de jure* participation score of more than 'four' for workers over the set of sixteen decisions, compared to an average of 2.2 for the sample as a whole. When these two outlying cases are excluded from the analysis the PS coefficient for workers is no longer significant at the 5 per cent level and the adjusted R^2 drops close to zero.

These results are not incompatible with the operation of a threshold effect between *de jure* participation (PS) and influence (PO). They also suggest, however, that the PS results for workers in Table 4.3 need to be interpreted with caution since the impact of institutional norms on worker influence in 1987 may not be as strong as this table implies. Institutional norms may not, in fact, be any better predictors of patterns of worker influence in 1987 than in 1977.

By and large, institutional norms also do not appear to be any better predictors of the influence of internal management groups in 1987 than in 1977. The institutional framework for participation does, however, hold up as a reasonable predictor of the overall distribution of influence between management and labour (M-W and M-R) in 1987. In 1987, like in 1977, institutional norms which inhibit the participation of management groups in organizational decision-making while promoting that of workers and their representatives, tend to contribute to a greater equalization of influence in organizations, with formal norms having a particularly significant effect on the distribution of influence between management and representative bodies at the plant (Table 4.3).

Impact of Unemployment

The situation in respect of the unemployment variable is more complex than for the PS variable. Comparison of Tables 4.2 and 4.3 shows that, by and large, the 1987 unemployment results for internal management groups (levels B, C, and D) parallel those for 1977. In 1987, like in 1977, the impact of the unemployment variable is restricted primarily to top management (level D). In both time-periods unemployment tends to enhance the overall influence of this group over organizational decisions. But in 1987 the effect of the unemployment variable, though significant, is small in magnitude. On the whole, therefore, the impact of unemployment on top management does not appear to be as marked in 1987 as in 1977.

More importantly, the results in Table 4.3 seem to suggest that in 1987 the unemployment rate no longer is a significant predictor of the influence of either workers or representative bodies at the plant. The same applies in respect of the distribution of influence between management and labour (M-W and M-R). As noted above though, some of these results may not be all that robust. Before we can draw any conclusions about the possible effects of unemployment on labour in 1987 we need to consider the fuller set of regression results for this period presented in Appendix B. Close inspection of these results confirms the lack of a significant association for the 1987 data between the rate of unemployment and the overall influence of representative bodies at the plant. It also confirms the lack of an association between the unemployment rate and the overall distribution of influence between management and workers for 1987 (M-W). The data in Appendix B also suggest, however, that in 1987, like in 1977, unemployment tends to have a negative effect on workers' influence. Though significant, this effect appears to be relatively weak, probably weaker than in 1977. The same applies in respect of the impact of unemployment on the overall distribution of influence between management and representative bodies at the plant (M-R).

In brief, our analysis suggests that for internal management groups as well as for workers the 1977 unemployment results by and large reappear in 1987. The relationship between the general state of the labour-market and patterns of influence for these groups tends to be fairly stable over time, although the impact of unemployment appears, on the whole, to be slightly weaker in 1987 than in 1977. For representative bodies, on the other hand, the picture is different. The results for this key group are the only ones that show definite signs of instability over time, with unemployment appearing to have a much weaker impact on the influence of worker representatives in 1987 than in 1977. Because of the unexpected nature of this finding and because of the importance of representative bodies from the point of view of the debate on industrial democracy, the discrepancy between 1977 and 1987 results for this group is worth closer investigation.

Unemployment and the Influence of Representative Bodies

Local Labour Market Argument. There are a number of possible explanations for this finding. One explanation is in terms of variations in local labour-market conditions within the countries covered in our study. This explanation rests on two interrelated arguments or hypotheses:

(i) that the influence of worker representatives at the level of the enterprise is more directly affected by the state of the local labour-market than by the rate of unemployment in the economy as a whole; and

(ii) that there are greater within-country variations in local labour-market conditions across our sample in 1987 than in 1977.

Taken together these two factors would help to explain why the relationship between the rate of unemployment and trade union influence was found to be significantly weaker in 1987 than in 1977. Unfortunately we are not in a position to test the second of these two hypotheses. As part of the 1987 study we did, however, collect some local labour-market information relevant to testing the first hypothesis.

In 1987, key management and worker representatives in each organization were asked to assess (on a four-point scale) how easy or difficult it was: (*a*) to fill vacancies for skilled, semi-skilled, and unskilled jobs respectively at the plant, and (*b*) for each type of worker (skilled, semi-skilled, and unskilled) to find an equivalent job in the area. The answers on these items were then combined into an overall measure of the state of the local labour market as perceived by management and worker representatives at the plant—the higher the score the tighter the local labour-market. In order to test our first hypothesis, this new local labour-market variable was added to our standard 'institutional–economic–contextual' model and the 1987 regressions were then recomputed using this extended model. In line with the hypothesis, the results of this analysis suggest that the state of the local labour-market is indeed a more important determinant of the influence of worker representatives at the plant than is the general rate of unemployment.[6] Unlike the un-employment variable, the new labour-market variable was found to have a significant positive impact on representative bodies, suggesting that a tight local labour-market tends to enhance the overall influence of this group over organizational decisions. This new variable also emerged as an important predictor of the relative influence of manage-ment and representative bodies at the level of the enterprise, with a tight labour-market tending, as expected, to be associated with a more equal distribution of influence between management and labour.

Lacking the data necessary to test the second part of the local labour-market argument outlined above, we are not in a position either defin-itely to reject or accept this argument as a possible explanation for the different unemployment results which were obtained for representative bodies in 1977 and 1987. All we can conclude from our additional ana-lysis is that local labour-market conditions are indeed important in explaining variations in trade union influence at the level of the enter-prise and that, consequently, the argument from the local labour-market can by no means be ignored. But the overall validity of this argument remains open to question.

Conflict Argument. A second potential explanation for the different un-employment results obtained for representative bodies in the two time-periods is in terms of conflict. The basic argument here is that unemployment, for a number of reasons, tends to weaken the relative bargaining-power of representative bodies at the level of the plant there-by reducing their *potential* influence within the enterprise. But repres-entatives' *actual* influence over decision-making is likely to depend, at least in part, on the extent to which their interests or preferences over particular issues either coincide or conflict with those of management. The greater the conflict of interest between management and labour, the greater is the likelihood that management will seek, and be able, to take advantage of its superior bargaining-position to influence decision out-

---

[6] The details of this analysis for the total decision set are available from the IDE Group upon request.

comes in line with its own preferences, and/or to centralize control over decision-making in its own hands. In either case labour's influence can be expected to be lower than in situations where there is a greater perceived congruence of interests between management and labour. The more consensual the plant-level system of industrial relations, therefore, the weaker can the relationship between unemployment and the influence of representative bodies be expected to be.

This contingency type argument which treats conflict/consensus as a moderator variable modifying the nature of the relationship between unemployment and influence, can be applied to our data with a view to explaining the observed discrepancies between the 1977 and 1987 unemployment results for representative bodies. More specifically, the explanation from conflict rests on two interrelated hypotheses:

(i) that the impact of unemployment on the influence of representative bodies is weaker in more consensual than in more conflictual plant-level systems of industrial relations; and

(ii) that for our sample as a whole there has been a move from more to less conflictual plant-level systems of labour-management relations between 1977 and 1987.

Once again we are not in a position to test the second of these two hypotheses since no conflict data are available for 1977. In 1987, however, we asked key management respondents and worker representatives in each organization whether each of the sixteen decisions in our decision set usually involved conflicts or disagreements. The answers over the sixteen decisions were then combined into an overall measure of decision-making conflict in the organization as perceived by management and worker representatives at the plant—the higher the score, the more conflictual the organization. Using this new conflict variable the first hypothesis above was examined by dividing the 1987 sample into two groups comprising high- and low-conflict organizations respectively. We then tested for the impact of unemployment on worker representatives separately in each group to see whether it was indeed greater in low- than in high-conflict organizations. The results of this analysis failed to lend support to the hypothesis.[7] If anything, in fact, unemployment was found to have a stronger negative impact on the influence of representative bodies in low rather than in high conflict systems. It would appear, therefore, that the explanation from conflict can be discounted since this explanation ultimately depends on *both* hypotheses holding 'true'.

Institutional Framework Argument. A last potential explanation for the difference between the 1977 and 1987 unemployment result for

[7] Detailed results available from the IDE Group upon request.

representative bodies is in terms of the institutional framework for participation itself. Central to this explanation is the idea that institutional norms which promote and legitimate the participation of representative bodies in organizational decision-making, if sufficiently highly developed, can help to maintain or even enhance their influence over organizational decisions even in the face of potentially adverse economic conditions. According to this interpretation, institutional norms can dampen, or possibly even counteract, the effects of economic conditions on labour. The emphasis here, therefore, is on a contingency interpretation of our data with institutional factors helping to moderate the relationship between unemployment and influence. More specifically, the explanation from institutional norms, like the previous explanations, is based on two interrelated hypotheses:

(i) first, that the impact of unemployment on the influence of representative bodies varies depending on the institutional context—the more highly developed the institutional framework for participation, the weaker is the impact which general labour-market conditions are likely to have on worker representatives; and

(ii) secondly, that across our sample as a whole, there was a significant increase in the level of *de jure* participation for representative bodies between 1977 and 1987.

Taken together these two factors would help to account for the much weaker impact which the unemployment variable was found to have on the influence of representative bodies in 1987 than in 1977.

Looking at the second of these two hypotheses first, comparison of the 1977 and 1987 data confirms that the PS scores for representative bodies changed in the expected direction during this period. For the sample as a whole, the average *de jure* participation score for this group across the sixteen decisions increased from 2.78 to 3.06 (on the six-point PS scale) between 1976 and 1986. Although not very marked this difference is statistically significant (0.01 level). More importantly, the overall shape of the distribution on the PS variable changed considerably between the two periods (see Chapter 3). From the point of view of the present argument, what is particularly important is the fact that a far greater proportion of organizations fall at the higher end of the distribution in 1986 that in 1976. Thus, in 1976 only 32 per cent of the organizations in our sample had total PS scores above 'three' for representative bodies, compared to 59 per cent in 1986. (For scores greater than 'four' the comparable figures for 1976 and 1986 are 4 per cent and 22 per cent respectively.)

Although central to the overall argument from institutional norms outlined above, this upward shift in the distribution of PS scores cannot, on its own, be used to 'explain' the different unemployment results which were obtained for representative bodies in the two time-periods. For this we must look also at the first contingency hypothesis outlined above, testing it against independent data. In order to do this the 1986 sample was first divided into two groups consisting of organizations with high and low PS scores respectively for representative bodies, using the mean on the PS variable as the cut-off point. The influence (PO) score for representative bodies was then regressed on to the unemployment variable for each group of organizations separately. The same procedure was followed for the 1976 data, this time, though, excluding the Yugoslav cases from the analysis for the reason already outlined above.

The results of this analysis do not lend much support to the contingency hypothesis.[8] On the basis of this hypothesis we would expect to find a stronger (negative) relationship between unemployment and influence among the low rather than the high PS organizations. Instead, for 1977 the actual and predicted results go in the opposite direction. This may be due to the generally low levels of *de jure* participation in 1977 and to the relatively high concentration of cases in the lower–middle ranges of the PS scale. For these reasons, the 1977 data may not necessarily provide a 'fair' test of the contingency hypothesis. For 1987, the relationship between unemployment and influence is, as expected, weaker for the high than for the low PS organizations. For the latter group, however, the regression coefficient on the unemployment variable is positive rather than negative. This result may be mainly a function of country-specific effects. On the other hand, it clearly goes against the thrust of the contingency argument outlined above and, consequently, throws into question the overall validity of the explanation from institutional norms.

In brief, of the three main explanations considered, the one from the local labour-market appears to be the most promising in helping to account for the differential impact which the rate of unemployment was found to have on the influence of representative bodies in 1977 and 1987. The two more complex contingency explanations in terms of conflict and the institutional framework for participation did not find clear support in our data. However, even the local labour-market explanation must remain tentative. At the end of the day, on the basis of our data we are not in a position to provide a fully satisfactory explanation for the 1987 findings relating to the unemployment variable.

Impact of Contextual Variables

Turning to the last set of independent variables in our model, Table 4.3 suggests that the impact of contextual variables on patterns of influence

---

[8] Detailed results available from the IDE Group upon request.

TABLE 4.4. *Cross-Sectional Analysis of 1977 and 1987 Data: Impact of Independent Variables on Patterns of Influence (PO) in 1977 and 1987, by Level*

Regression	Relationship between Independent Variables and Influence (PO)								
	De-jure Part (PS)			Unemployment rate			Contextual variables		
Equations	1977	1987	Stability	1977	1987	Stability	1977	1987	Stability
Workers(A)	NS	NS	Stable/NS	Sig(−)	Sig(−)	Stable/Sig	Sig(+)	NS	Unstable
Supervisor(B)	NS	NS	Stable/NS	NS	NS	Stable/NS	Sig(−)	NS	Unstable
Middle management(C)	NS	NS	Stable/NS	NS	NS	Stable/NS	NS	NS	Stable/NS
Top management (D)	NS	NS	Stable/NS	Sig(+)	Sig(+)	Stable/Sig	Sig(−/+)	NS	Unstable
Representative Bodies (F)	Sig(+)	Sig(+)	Stable/Sig	Sig(−)	NS	Unstable	NS	NS	Stable/NS
Management-workers (M-W)	Sig(−)	NS	Unstable	Sig(−)	NS	Unstable	NS	NS	Stable/NS
Management-representatives (M-R)	Sig(+)	Sig(+)	Stable/Sig	Sig(+)	Sig(+)	Stable/Sig	Sig(−)	Sig(−)	Unstable/Sig

Key:
Sig = Relationship between dependent and independent variable significant at <5% level.
NS = Relationship between dependent and independent variable not significant at 5% level.
(+) = Significant positive relationship.
(−) = Significant negative relationship.
Stable/Sig = Strength and direction of relationship between dependent and independent variable stable over time and significant in both 1977 and 1987.
Stable/NS = Strength and direction of relationship between dependent and variable stable over time but not significant in either 1977 or 1987.
Unstable = Strength and direction of relationship between dependent and independent variable unstable over time.
Unstable/Sig = Relationship significant in both 1977 and 1987 but involving different contextual variables in each period.

in organizations tends to be even weaker in 1987 than in 1977. For 1987 there is some evidence that 'functional differentiation' tends to enhance the overall influence of representative bodies relative to management groups at the plant. There is also some evidence that 'formal independence' (i.e. organizational autonomy) tends to be associated with higher overall levels of influence for top management (Level D). Apart from specific and rather limited effects of this kind, however, none of the contextual variables which attained significance in the 1977 analysis consistently shows up as significant predictors of influence in 1987. In particular, structural characteristics of the enterprise which were found to have a significant impact on both the absolute and relative influence of management groups in 1977, such as the degree of formalization of the organization, no longer appear to be significant in 1987.

Summary of Cross-Sectional Analyses of 1977 and 1987 Data

Given the results on both the contextual and the unemployment variables, it is not surprising to find that our mixed model incorporating institutional, economic, and contextual factors tends to perform less well overall on the 1987 than on the 1977 data. Comparison of the adjusted R^2 figures for the 1977 and 1987 regressions shows that, on the whole, our model tends to account for a higher proportion of the variance in patterns of influence in organizations in 1977 than in 1987. The difference in this respect is most noticeable in relation to top management but is apparent also across other management levels, as well as in relation to the overall distribution of influence between management and workers (M-W).

More generally, as we have seen, comparison of the 1977 and 1987 data reveals quite a complex pattern across the two time-periods and points to important differences as well as similarities between the 1977 and 1987 results. The main results of the 1977 and 1987 analyses are summarized, in simplified form, in Table 4.4. For each of the three main types of independent variables in our model (i.e. institutional, economic, and contextual factors), the figure shows: (*a*) whether the variable in question was found to have a significant impact on the influence of each level in 1977 and 1987 respectively, (*b*) the direction of the relationship (positive or negative) for those variables attaining at least the 5 per cent level of significance, (*c*) whether the relationship is stable over time (i.e. whether the strength and direction of the relationship are the same in 1977 and 1987), and (*d*) if the relationship is stable, whether it is significant in both time-periods. The entries for 1977 are based on the results of the 1977 analysis presented in Table 4.2, while the 1987 entries incorporate the results both of the 1987 analysis presented in Table 4.3, and of the further analysis and discussion of the 1987 data reported in the body of the chapter and in Appendix B.

The individual 1977 and 1987 results reported in Table 4.4 have already been discussed at some length above and will not be examined again in detail at this point. Here we shall limit ourselves to summarizing the most salient findings to emerge from the overall comparison of the 1977 and 1987 data reported in the figure. Three main points stand out in this respect. The first concerns the stability of the observed relationships over time. As can be seen from Table 4.4, for most levels (A to M-R) the 1977 results on both the PS and the unemployment variables reappear in 1987, suggesting that, on the whole, the relationship between patterns of influence and both institutional norms and the general state of the labour-market tends to be fairly stable over time. In contrast, the relationship between the contextual variables and the distribution of influence appears to be relatively unstable with the strength and/or direction of the impact of specific variables changing over time in four of the seven regression equations examined.

The second point concerns the strength of the observed relationships and the relative importance of institutional, economic, and contextual factors as overall predictors of patterns of influence distribution in organizations in the two time-periods. As can be seen from Table 4.4, of the independent variables in our model, only the institutional framework for participation and the unemployment rate emerge as significant determinants of patterns of influence in both 1977 and 1987. The PS variable attains significance in both 1977 and 1987 in two out of the seven regression equations examined (for level F and M-R), while the unemployment variable attains significance in three of the regressions (for levels A, D, and M-R), although, as we have seen, the impact of unemployment does not, on the whole, appear to be as marked in 1987 as in 1977. In contrast, none of the contextual variables which attained significance in the 1977 regression, including various structural characteristics of the enterprise, reappear as significant predictors of influence in 1987. Of the independent variables examined, therefore, only the institutional framework for participation and the general state of the labour-market were found to have a consistent and significant effect on the distribution of influence, thereby confirming the importance of both institutional and economic factors as determinants of patterns of influence in organizations, as well as highlighting the generally more limited role played by contextual factors in this respect.

Finally, turning to the results for the different groups (A to M-R), Table 4.4 shows that, taking into account both the 1977 and 1987 results, the institutional framework for participation emerges as the single most important predictor of the influence of representative bodies at the plant. For 1987, in fact, the PS Variable is the only significant predictor of the influence of representative bodies suggesting that for this group, most of the variance explained by our model in 1987 is attributable to institutional factors, with the unemployment rate and contextual variables adding little or nothing to the overall explanatory power of the model. The best overall predictor for workers, on the other hand, is the unemployment rate which, as expected, has a negative impact on the influence of this group in both time-periods. The unemployment rate is also the only factor which has a significant impact on the influence of top management in both 1977 and 1987, although for this group the effect, as expected, is in a positive direction. As we have seen, however, for managerial groups as a whole the explanatory power of our model tends to be rather limited, particularly in 1987. Finally, as far as the relative influence measures are concerned, the distribution of influence between management and representative bodies at the plant appears to be a function mainly of two factors, the institutional framework for participation and the unemployment rate. These two factors also appear to have some effect on the distribution of influence between management and workers in organizations, although in this case the impact is less pronounced, particularly in 1987.

LONGITUDINAL ANALYSIS

The Pattern over Time: Longitudinal Analysis of the 1977 and 1987 Data

So far, in this chapter, we have concentrated on a cross- sectional analysis and comparison of the 1977 and 1987 data. The determinants of influence were explored by first looking at the 1977 and then at the 1987 data and by then comparing the pattern of results across the two time-periods. In this section, we turn to a longitudinal analysis of the data and examine the extent to which changes in patterns of influence over time are related to changes in some of the key independent variables in our model, using the combined 1977 and 1987 data as the basis for our analysis. More specifically, the aim of this section is to explain changes in patterns of influence distribution in organizations between 1977 and 1987 and, in particular, to explore the extent to which such changes can be explained by reference to changes in institutional norms and in the general state of the labour-market in the ten-year period under consideration. As part of this analysis we will introduce some additional variables into our model and test a number of alternative 'longitudinal' versions of this new model on the combined 1977 and 1987 data. In the process, we will try to provide an overall interpretation of the IDE data, taking into account the results of both the cross-sectional and longitudinal analyses.

TABLE 4.5. *Extended Analysis of 1987 Data: Regressions of 1987 Influence Scores (PO 1987) on to 1977 Influence Scores (PO 1977) and other Variables (1987) for the Total Decision Set, by Level*

Predictors	Regression Equations (A to M-R)						
	A Influence workers	B Influence supervisors	C Influence middle management	D Influence top management	F Influence representative bodies	M-W Influence management-workers	M-R Influence management-representatives
1977 Influence (PO) Score per Level (A to M-R)	+	–	+	0.25	0.52	0.30	0.60
1987 PS Score per Level (A to M-R)	0.52*		+	0.25	0.28	+	0.21
Unemployment Rate(87)	–	–	–	0.31	–	+	
Formal Independence (87)	+	–	–	–		–	+
Skill Requirements (87)		–					
Product Complexity (87)	+	+	+				
Functional Difference(87)	+	+	+		+	–	–
Adjusted R^2	0.24	0	0.03	0.12	0.57	0.16	0.56
(N)	(66)	(60)	(60)	(66)	(61)	(66)	(61)

Key: as in Table 4.1 for all variables except for 1977 Influence (PO) Scores.
1977 Influence (PO) Scores used as Predictors of 1987 Influence (PO) Scores in Equations A to M-R.
Equations A, B, C, D, and F: Mean 1977 influence score of levels A, B, C, D, and F respectively over set of 16 decisions.
Equation M-W: Mean 1977 influence score of three management groups over 16 decisions minus mean 1977 influence score of workers over 16 decisions.
Equation M-R: Mean 1977 influence score of three management groups over 16 decisions minus mean 1977 influence score of representative bodies over 16 decisions.

* Numbers in table are standardized regression coefficients.

Relationship between 1977 and 1987 Patterns of Influence

We start by computing a new model for the 1987 data using the influence (PO) scores for 1977 as co-predictors of influence in 1987. The aim of this analysis is to see whether 1987 influence patterns were conditioned not only by the particular economic conditions and institutional arrangements for participation which obtained at the time, as our cross-sectional analysis suggests, but also by 'historical' patterns of influence distribution, i.e. by the particular patterns which obtained in 1977. More generally, the aim is to see whether, in the organizations covered in our study, there was a tendency for the patterns of influence distribution which obtain in the late 1970s to reproduce themselves over time and to survive into the late 1980s. To test for this, the 1977 influence (PO) scores for each level over the total decision set were added as predictor variables to our standard institutional–economic–contextual model for 1987. The 1987 regressions reported in Table 4.3 were then recomputed using this extended version of the model. The results of this analysis are reported in Table 4.5.

Comparison of Tables 4.3 and 4.5 shows that the introduction of the 1977 influence variables into the 1987 regressions does not, by and large, greatly affect the results for the institutional, economic, and contextual variables. In terms of its overall explanatory power, however, the new model seems to perform better than the old one, at least for top management and for representative bodies, as well as for the two relative influence measures (see adjusted R^2 for levels D, F, M-W, and M-R in Tables 4.3 and 4.5). Inspection of Table 4.5 shows that for these groups, the 1977 influence variable is a significant predictor of patterns of influence in 1987. The impact is particularly marked for representative bodies (level F) and for the relative influence between management and both workers and their representatives at the plant (M-W and M-R). In all cases the impact is positive indicating that, in organizations where management or labour groups were influential in 1977 they tended to remain so also in 1987, while where they were weak, they tended to remain weak. More generally, these results point to a fair degree of stability, or even inertia, in patterns of influence distribution over time with groups who were influential in 1977 managing to take advantage of their superior position to retain, or even increase, their influence in 1987. In turn, this dynamic may help to account for the fact that, despite the recessionary pressures of the 1980s and the sharp increase in unemployment which took place during this period, labour's influence over organizational decisions does not, on the whole, appear to have declined between 1977 and 1987 (see Chapter 3). In order to examine this proposition we need, however, to adopt a more explicitly longitudinal approach to the data and look at the determinants of changes in patterns of influence distribution over time. It is to this analysis, therefore, that we now turn.

Determinants of Changes in Patterns of Influence over Time

In the following analysis, changes in patterns of influence distribution between 1977 and 1987 will be related to three main factors: (1) changes in patterns of *de jure* participation (PS) between the two time-periods, (2) changes in the general rate of unemployment between 1977 and 1987, and (3) 'historical' patterns of influence distribution, i.e. the amount of influence exercised by different groups over organizational decisions in 1977. Contextual variables have been excluded from the analysis for two reasons. First, preliminary analysis of the combined 1977 and 1987 data showed, as expected, none of the contextual variables to be significant predictors of changes in patterns of influence over time. Second, because of missing data on these variables for both 1977 and 1987, their inclusion in the regression equations tends to reduce substantially the number of observations in the analysis. On balance, therefore, it was thought best to exclude the contextual variables altogether from the longitudinal analysis and concentrate only on the three main institutional, economic, and 'historical' factors identified above as potential predictors of changes in patterns of influence between 1977 and 1987.

In order to simplify the discussion we also decided to restrict our analysis to those aspects of the distribution of influence which are central to the debate on industrial democracy focusing, in particular, on the determinants of changes in the position of labour within the enterprise over the ten-year period under consideration. In the following analysis, therefore, we will restrict our attention to workers and representative bodies at the plant (levels A and F), and to the two relative influence measures (M-W and M-R) designed to assess the overall distribution of influence between management and labour in organizations. Changes in the overall position of the three main management groups within the enterprise (i.e. supervisors and middle and top management) will be examined through the relative influence measures, but no separate analyses will be presented for each of these three groups. Note also that as part of this analysis a number of new 'change variables' were constructed designed to measure differences in the rate of unemployment and in the level of influence (PO) and of *de jure* participation (PS) of the different groups between 1977 and 1987. In all cases the new change measures were constructed by subtracting the 1977 from the 1987 values on the relevant variables. A positive score on the new change measures indicates that there has been an increase in the value of the variable between the two time-periods, while a negative score indicates that the variable has decreased over time. The main dependent and independent

Dependent Variables

Change in Influence (PO) Score per Level (1987–1977 scores)

– Change in Influence of Workers (Level A)
– Change in Influence of Representative Bodies (Level F)
– Change in Relative Influence of Management and Workers (M-W)
– Change in Relative Influence of Management and Representative Bodies (M-R)

Independent Variables

1. Institutional (PS) Variables

    Change in de jure Participation (PS) Score per Level (1987–1977 Scores)

    – Change in *de jure* Participation of Workers (Level A)
    – Change in *de jure* Participation of Representative Bodies (Level F)
    – Change in Relative *de jure* Participation of Management and Workers (M-W)
    – Change in Relative *de jure* Participation of Management and Representative Bodies (M-R)

2. Macro-economic Variables

    – Change in overall rate of unemployment (1987–1977 scores)

3. 'Historical' Patterns of Influence Distribution

    1977 Influence (PO) Scores per Level

    – Influence of Workers in 1977 (Level A)
    – Influence of Representative Bodies in 1977 (Level F)
    – Relative Influence of Management and Workers in 1977 (M-W)
    – Relative Influence of Management and Representative Bodies in 1977 (M–R)

Fig. 4.2 Dependent and Independent Variables Used in the Multivariate Longitudinal Analysis of the Combined 1977 and 1987 IDE Data

variables used in the longitudinal analysis of the combined 1977 and 1987 data are shown in Figure 4.2.

From our previous discussion and the results of the analysis presented so far in this chapter, we would expect to find a negative association between changes in unemployment and changes in both the absolute and relative influence of workers and their representatives at the plant between 1977 and 1987. More specifically an increase in unemployment can be expected to weaken the bargaining-power of labour *vis-à-vis* management, thereby reducing its overall influence over organizational decisions, while at the same time increasing that of management. By the same token, a decrease in unemployment can be expected to have the opposite effect on the position of labour. Similarly, for workers and representative bodies, we would expect to find a positive association between changes in pattern of *de jure* participation (PS) and influence

(PO) between 1977 and 1987, with the introduction of new institutional norms which legitimate the participation of labour groups in organizational decisions and give them greater access to decision-making processes within the enterprise, helping to strengthen both their absolute and relative influence within the organization.

In contrast, the relationship between 1977 patterns of influence distribution and subsequent changes in the absolute and relative influence of labour over organization decisions, is potentially more complex. Two competing arguments or hypotheses can be identified in this respect. The first argument is in terms of what might be called 'system inertia' or 'power accumulation' and echoes our previous discussion on this point. According to this argument, the greater the influence of a particular group at a given point in time, the better placed it is likely to be to defend, or even to improve, its position in the future. By the same token, the less influential the group, the less likely it is that it will be able to defend, let alone improve, its position in the future. Other things being equal, therefore, we would expect to find a positive relationship between the amount of absolute and relative influence exercised by labour groups in 1977 and changes in their influence over time, with the position of groups which were more influential in 1977 tending to improve over the ten-year period under consideration, and those of groups which were weaker tending to deteriorate.

The second argument is in terms of what might be called 'management strategy'. It focuses primarily on the behaviour and reactions of management and leads to opposite predictions to those of the first argument outlined above. The management strategy argument is based on the assumption that it is in management's interest to ensure that workers and their representative within the enterprise do not exercise too much influence over organizational decisions. It follows from this that management is more likely to want to contain and, if possible, to reduce the influence of strong rather than of weak groups. It is the former groups, in fact, which are most likely to be able to challenge management's authority and prerogatives within the enterprise and which are, therefore, most likely to preoccupy management. Below a certain level of influence, management is likely to be relatively indifferent to the position of labour. More generally, therefore, the greater the influence of labour at a particular point in time, the keener management is likely to be to weaken or undermine its position in the future. Other things being equal, therefore, we would expect to find a negative rather than a positive relationship between the amount of influence exercised by labour groups in 1977 and changes in their influence over time. This relationship, however, can be expected to be more marked, or to hold primarily, in organizations where workers and representative bodies enjoyed relatively high levels of influence in 1977. According to the management strategy argument, in fact, it is in these organizations that management is likely to have been particularly keen to curtail the influence of labour and where, therefore, the position of workers and representative bodies can be expected to have deteriorated most markedly after 1977. In contrast, in organizations where labour was already relatively weak in 1977 and where management can, therefore, be expected to have been relatively indifferent to the situation, the pattern of change after 1977 is not likely to be as clear, thereby making the relationship more indeterminate.

General Explanatory Models of Influence

Based on the above discussion, two general explanatory models of influence can be distinguished—a 'power accumulation/system inertia' model and a 'management strategy' model. Both models are designed to explain changes in the absolute and relative influence of workers and representative bodies between 1977 and 1987, but are based on different premises and lead to different predictions and interpretations of the data. A schematic representation of the two models is shown in Figure 4.3.

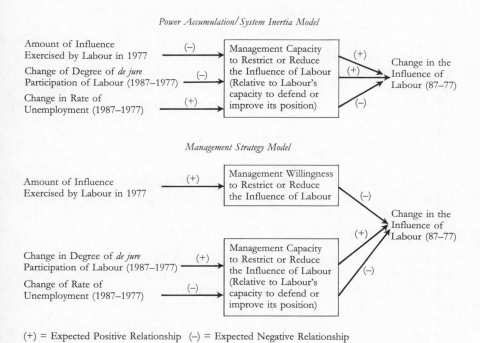

Fig. 4.3 Alternative Explanatory Models of Influence

According to the power accumulation/system inertia model, shifts in the influence of labour between 1977 and 1987 are primarily a function of management's capacity to contain or reduce its influence within the enterprise over the period under consideration (relative to labour's capacity to defend or improve its position). In turn, this capacity is a function of a number of more specific factors including, not only changes in institutional and economic conditions between 1977 and 1987, but also the amount of influence exercised by labour at the beginning of the period under consideration. In line with our previous discussion, therefore, changes in the influence of labour over time can, according to this model, be expected to be negatively related to changes in the unemployment rate, but positively related both to changes in the institutional framework for participation (PS) and to the amount of influence exercised by labour in 1977.

In contrast, the management strategy model views shifts in the position of labour groups within the enterprise as a function not only of management's capacity to contain or reduce their influence over time, but also of its willingness to do so. In turn, management's willingness to act depends on how much influence labour had within the enterprise to start with, while its capacity to act is a function of institutional and economic conditions. According to this model, therefore, changes in the influence of labour can, as before, be expected to be negatively related to changes in the unemployment rate and positively related to changes in the PS variable. However, in line with our previous argument from management strategy, the amount of influence exercised by labour in 1977 can, in this case, be expected to be negatively rather than positively related to subsequent changes in its position within the enterprise (see Fig. 4.3).

The main predictions associated with the two models can be summarized in the following set of hypotheses.

Hypothesis 1. The greater the increase in the absolute and relative degrees of *de jure* participation (PS) of labour in organizational decisions between 1977 and 1987, the greater the increase in its absolute and relative influence between the two time-periods.

Hypothesis 2. The greater the increase in the general rate of unemployment between 1977 and 1987, the greater the decrease in the absolute and relative influence of labour over organizational decisions between the two time-periods.

Hypothesis 3(a). The greater the absolute and relative influence of labour over organizational decisions in 1977, the greater the *increase* in its absolute and relative influence between 1977 and 1987.

Hypothesis 3(b). The greater the absolute and relative influence of labour over organizational decisions in 1977, the greater the *decrease* in its absolute and relative influence between 1977 and 1987.

Hypotheses 1 and 2 apply to both models. Hypothesis 3(*a*) on the other hand, is linked specifically to the power accumulation model, while hypothesis 3(*b*) is linked to the management strategy model. Note that, because of the way our relative influence measures were constructed, the direction of some of the above hypothesized relationships can be expected to be reversed in the empirical analysis of the data. To facilitate comparison with the actual results of the analysis which will be presented below, the expected direction of the relationship between each of the dependent and independent variables in the two models, taking into account the way in which specific variables were constructed, is summarized in Table 4.6.

As noted above, according to the management strategy argument, the overall relationship between the amount of influence exercised by labour groups in 1976 and subsequent changes in their influence over organizational decisions, can be expected to be negative. As we have seen, though, this relationship can be expected to be more pronounced in organizations where labour enjoyed a generally stronger position in 1976 (see discussion on page 1). This points to an additional hypothesis linked specifically to the management strategy model.

Hypothesis 4. The strength of the (negative) relationship between 1976 patterns of influence distribution and changes in the absolute and relative influence of labour between 1976 and 1986 varies depending on the amount of influence exercised by labour at the beginning of the period under consideration—the greater the influence of labour in 1976, the stronger the (negative) relationship between the above variables can be expected to be. This hypothesis is essentially a more refined contingent version of hypothesis 3(*b*).

Finally, it is important to note that, by linking changes in the position of labour to both management's capacity and willingness to act, the management strategy model directs attention also to some potentially more complex interactive effects between variables. In particular, the model suggests that whether or not increases in the rate of unemployment, or decreases in the degree of *de jure* participation of workers and representative bodies, actually lead to decreases in their influence over organizational decisions depends, at least in part, on management's willingness or desire to take advantage of the opportunities provided by these changes to undermine or weaken labour's position within the enterprise. In turn, this willingness is a function of the amount of influence exercised by labour at the beginning of the period under consideration. The greater the influence of labour in 1977, the greater is the

TABLE 4.6. *Expected Direction of Relationship between Dependent and Independent Variables in Empirical Analysis of Alternative Models of Influence, by Level*

Independent variables	Power Accumulation/System Inertia Model (Dependent Variables)			
	A Change in influence of workers (1987–1977)	F Change in influence representative bodies (1987–1977)	M-W Change in relative influence management-workers (1987–1977)	M-R Change in relative influence management-representatives (1987–1977)
Change in PS score per level (1987–1977)	+	+	+	+
Change in unemployment (1987–1977)	–	–	+	+
1977 Influence (PO) score per level	+	+	+	+
Management Strategy Model (Dependent Variables)				
Change in PS score per level (1987–1977)	+		+	+
Change in unemployment (1987–1977)	–		+	+
1977 Influence (PO) score per level	–		–	–

Key:
+ = Expected Positive Relationship between variables
– = Expected Negative Relationship between variables

likelihood that management will seek to take advantage of new opportunities created by changes in institutional arrangements and/or in the general state of the labour-market, to reassert its authority within the enterprise and centralize control over decision-making in its own hands. The greater the influence of labour in 1977, therefore, the stronger can the relationship between the remaining independent and dependent variables in the model be expected to be.

This contingency-type argument which treats the amount of influence exercised by labour in 1977 as a moderator variable modifying the nature of the relationship between the other variables in the model, points to a last set of hypotheses linked specifically to the management strategy model:

Hypotheses 5(a) and (b). The impact of changes in institutional and economic conditions on the influence of labour varies depending on the amount of influence exercised by labour in 1977—the greater the influence of labour groups in 1977, the stronger is the impact which subsequent (unfavourable) changes in (*a*) institutional norms and (*b*) in the general state of the labour-market are likely to have on their absolute and relative influence over organizational decisions.

Hypotheses 5(*a*) and (*b*) are more refined contingent versions of hypotheses 1 and 2 respectively.

Tests of Alternative Models of Influence

The power-accumulation and management-strategy models were tested against the combined 1977 and 1987 data by regressing the change in the influence score for each level between 1977 and 1987 on to the three main predictor variables included in the models (see Figs. 4.2 and 4.3 above). The results of this analysis, designed to test hypothesis 1, 2, 3(*a*), and 3(*b*), are shown in Table 4.7.

Inspection of the table shows that the 1977 influence variable is a major predictor of changes in both the absolute and relative influence of labour over organizational decisions between 1977 and 1987. This finding is in line with the predictions of both models. In all cases, however, the impact is negative rather than positive, thereby confirming hypothesis 3(*b*) and lending support to the management-strategy rather than to the power-accumulation model (see Table 4.6). That is to say, the results of the analysis fail to support the power-accumulation argument and point instead to the alternative interpretation in terms-management strategy.

Hypothesis 2 also finds strong support in the data. As can be seen from Table 4.7, the unemployment variable emerges as a significant determinant of the influence of both workers and representative bodies between 1977 and 1987. In all cases the impact is in the expected direction with

TABLE 4.7. *Analysis of Combined 1977 and 1987 Data: Regressions of Changes in Influence (PO 1987–PO 1977) on to Changes in other Variables (1987–1977) and 1977 Influence Scores (PO 1977) for the Total Decision Set, by Level. (Tests of Hypothesis 1, 2, 3(a), and 3(b))*

Predictors	Regression Equations (A, F, M-W, and M-R)			
	A Change in influence (PO) workers (1987–1977)	F Change in influence (PO) representative bodies (1987–1977)	M-W Change in relative influence (PO) management-workers (1987–1977)	M-R Change in relative influence management-representatives (1987–1977)
Change in PS score per level (1987–1977)	0.20*	–	+	+
Change in unemployment (1987–1977)	– 0.29	– 0.36	0.36	0.24
1977 influence (PO) score per level	– 0.57	– 0.34	– 0.59	– 0.35
Adjusted R²	0.33	0.15	0.31	0.10
(N)	(87)	(86)	(87)	(86)

Key:
PS Measures used as Predictors of Changes in PO in Equations A, F, M-W, M-R
Equations A and F: 1987–1977 PS score of levels A and F respectively.
Equation M-W: 1987–1977 Relative PS score of management and workers.
Equation M-R: 1987–1977 Relative PS score of management and representative bodies.

1977 PO Scores used as Predictors of Changes in PO in Equations A, F, M-W, M-R
Equations A and F: 1977 PO score for levels A and F respectively.
Equation M-W: 1977 Relative PO score of management and workers.
Equation M-R: 1977 Relative PO score of management and representative bodies.

* Numbers in the table are standardized regression coefficients.

increasing unemployment tending to reduce both the absolute and relative influence of labour groups within the enterprise (see also Table 4.6). In contrast, support for hypothesis 1 appears to be more limited. The institutional framework for participation (PS) tends, in fact, to be a weaker predictor of changes in influence than are either of the other two variables included in the analysis. Nor is the impact of the PS variable always in the expected direction. Thus, as can be seen from Table 4.7, this variable emerges as a significant predictor of influence in only one of the four regression equations examined, that for workers, while in the equation for representative bodies the coefficient is negative rather than positive (see also Table 4.6).

In brief, therefore, the longitudinal analysis presented above leads to different conclusions from those of the cross-sectional analysis concerning the relative importance of institutional norms as predictors of the influence of labour over organizational decisions. In particular, the longitudinal analysis, unlike the cross-sectional analysis, suggests that the general state of the labour-market is a more important determinant of patterns of influence distribution in organizations than is the institutional framework for participation. At the same time, the longitudinal analysis also suggests that changes in patterns of labour influence between 1977 and 1987 were strongly affected by the nature of managerial strategies towards workers and their representatives at the plant. In turn, these strategies were conditioned by the nature of the 'pre-existing' system of industrial relations at the plant, and in particular by the 'pre-existing' distribution of influence between management and labour within the enterprise. As such, the results of the longitudinal analysis highlight the fact that shifts in the influence of labour between 1977 and 1987 can only be understood in historical perspective—by reference to the particular position enjoyed by management and labour in plant-level systems of industrial relations in the 1970s—and by taking into account the specific interests and strategies pursued by management within the enterprise during the period under consideration.

These general conclusions are confirmed and reinforced by an analysis of the three more complex contingency hypotheses identified above (hypotheses 4, 5(*a*), and 5(*b*). These three hypotheses were examined together by first dividing the organizations in the sample into two groups depending on the amount of absolute and relative influence exercised by workers and representative bodies in 1977. The first group consists of organizations with below-average 1977 influence (PO) scores for labour (type A), while the second group covers organizations with above-average scores for labour on the 1977 influence variable (type B). In other words, type A and type B organizations are ones where labour was relatively weak and strong respectively in 1977. The longitudinal regressions in Table 4.8, covering institutional, economic, and

TABLE 4.8. Analysis of Combined 1977 and 1987 Data: Regressions of Changes in Influence (PO 1987–PO 1977) on to Changes in other Variables (1987–1977) and 1977 Influence Scores (PO 1977) for the Total Decision Set, by Level. (Tests of Hypothesis 4 and 5)

Predictors	Regression Equations (A, F, M-W, and M-R)			
	A Changes in influence (PO) workers (1987–1977)	F Changes in influence (PO) representative bodies (1987–1977)	M-W Changes in relative influence (PO) management-workers (1987–1977)	M-R Changes in relative influence management-representatives (1987–1977)
Organizations with below Average 1977 PO Scores				
Change in PS score per level (1987–1977)	−	+	−	+
Change in unemployment (1987–1977)	−0.36	−	+	−
1977 Influence (PO) score per level	−	−	−0.40	−
Adjusted R^2	0.10	0.04	0.10	0
(N)	(44)	(45)	(39)	(44)
Significance	NS†	NS	NS	NS
Organizations with above Average 1977 PO Scores				
Change in PS score per level (1987–1977)	0.44	−0.32	+	−
Change in unemployment (1987–1977)	−0.31	−0.58	0.50	0.46
1977 Influence (PO) score per level	−0.38	−0.50	−0.59	−0.46
Adjusted R^2	0.35	0.42	0.38	0.26
(N)	(43)	(41)	(48)	(42)
Significance	0.000	0.000	0.000	0.002

Key: Same as in Table 4.7.
* Numbers in table are standardized regression coefficients
† NS = Overall equation not significant at 0.05 level

'historical' factors, were then recomputed separately for each sub-sample of organizations.[9] The results of this analysis are reported in Table 4.8.

The overall pattern of results lends strong support to a contingency interpretation of the data along the lines suggested by the three hypotheses. On the basis of these hypotheses we would expect our longitudinal model to work much better for type B than for type A organizations. Comparison of the adjusted R^2 figures in Table 4.8 confirms this. Moreover, as can be seen from the table, all the regression equations for type B organizations are significant while none of those for type A is. Linked to the above, ten out of the twelve coefficients in the second part of Table 4.8 are significant compared to only two in the first part, thereby lending further support to an overall contingency interpretation of the data.

As far as the individual hypotheses are concerned, comparison of the two parts of the table shows that hypothesis 4 is strongly supported by the data. On the basis of this hypothesis we would expect the 1977 influence variable to have a more marked negative impact on changes in the absolute and relative influence of labour between 1977 and 1987 in type B than in type A organizations. This is confirmed by our results. Thus, all of the coefficients for the 1977 variable for type B organizations are negative and significant, while for type A organizations only one of the coefficients is significant, that for the relative influence between management and workers (M-W). These results provide additional support for the management strategy argument and suggest that it was in organizations where labour had been relatively influential in the 1970s, rather than in those where it had been relatively weak to start with, that there was the greatest tendency for labour groups to loose ground to management during the 1980s.

Likewise, hypothesis 5(*b*) is also strongly supported by the data. In line with this hypothesis, all the coefficients for the unemployment variable for type B organizations are significant, while for type A organizations only the coefficient for workers is significant. Moreover, for type B organizations the impact for the unemployment variable is, in all cases, in the expected direction with a deterioration in the general state of the labour-market tending to reduce both the absolute and relative influence of labour groups within the enterprise. In this context it is important to note that, to a greater or lesser extent, all the countries in our sample

---

[9] The specific procedures used in this analysis were as follows: the sample was first divided into two groups consisting of organizations with low- and high-influence (PO) scores for workers in 1977, using the mean on the 1977 influence variable as the cut-off point. The longitudinal model comprising institutional, economic, and 'historical' variables was then tested seperately on each of the two sub-samples of organizations. The same procedure was then repeated for representative bodies and for the two relative influence measures.

experienced an increase in the rate of unemployment between 1977 and 1987 and that, in this respect, there is no significant difference between type A and type B organizations. In line with hypothesis 5(*b*) and the predictions of the management strategy model, therefore, the results of the analysis indicate that the impact of the unemployment variable does indeed vary depending on the amount of influence which labour groups exercised over organizational decisions in 1977. The stronger the position of labour in the 1970s, the greater was the tendency for management to take advantage of the general deterioration in the state of the labour-market which took place during the 1980s to reassert its authority within the enterprise and centralize control over decision-making more explicitly in its own hands.

In contrast, the results for the PS variable, which are linked to hypothesis 5(*a*), are less clear-cut. Inspection of Table 4.8 shows, as expected, that for type A organizations none of the coefficients for the PS variable is significant. For type B organizations, however, only two out of the four PS coefficients are significant, those for workers and for representative bodies. Moreover, the coefficient for the former group is positive while that for the latter is negative. These results may be a function of country-specific effects or, possibly, they may reflect the fact that some of the relationships involved may be non-monotonic. The key point to note though, is that the results in Table 4.8, like those of our previous longitudinal analysis, suggest that changes in the general state of the labour market between 1977 and 1987 tended, on the whole, to have a stronger effect on the influence of labour than did changes in institutional arrangements for participation.

In brief, the results of the longitudinal analysis suggest that patterns of influence distribution in organizations between 1977 and 1987 tended to be affected primarily by two factors, the amount of influence exercised by labour over organizational decisions in 1977 and subsequent changes in the general state of the labour-market. At the same time though, our analysis suggests that the changes in economic conditions which took place between 1976 and 1986 tended to have a differential impact on the position of labour groups within the enterprise depending on how influential these groups had been at the beginning of the period under consideration. In particular, our analysis suggests that labour is likely to have lost most ground in organizations where it had been relatively influential in the 1970s and where there subsequently was a sharp deterioration in the general state of the labour-market. That is to say, labour groups lost most ground in plant-level systems of industrial relations where management had a strong interest in reducing their influence over organizational decisions to start with, *and*, where changes in economic conditions subsequently enabled management to achieve its objectives (Type I Scenario).

At the opposite extreme are those systems where labour groups in the 1970s did not pose any particular threat to management's authority and prerogatives within the enterprise, *and*, where in the 1980s there was only a mild deterioration in the general state of the labour-market. These are the systems where labour's influence is least likely to have declined in the ten-year period under consideration (Type II Scenario). In some cases, in fact, labour's influence can be expected to have increased as a result of the introduction by management in the 1980s of various initiatives designed to make better use of human resources within the enterprise and to strengthen individual-organizational linkages, including, for example, quality circles, briefing groups, and various types of employee involvement programmes (Mileward and Stevens 1986; Batstone and Gourlay 1986; Kelly and Richardson 1989; Guest and Peccei 1992). These, however, were essentially management- rather than labour-driven changes introduced in systems characterized by historically low levels of labour influence and which did not, therefore, necessarily threaten management's control within the enterprise.

Between these two extremes are mixed situations where either (*a*) labour was relatively strong in the 1970s but where there was only a limited increase in unemployment in the 1980s, or (*b*) there was a sharp rise in unemployment in the 1980s but labour was relatively weak to start with and, therefore, never posed a particular threat to management (Type III Scenario). In these situations we would expect labour's influence to have remained relatively stable over time or, at least, not to have declined as much as in the first type of scenario identified above.

Table 4.9 gives a breakdown of the organizations in the sample in terms of the three main types of scenario discussed above and, for each group of organizations, shows the extent to which there was either an increase or a decrease in the absolute and relative influence of workers and representative bodies between 1977 and 1987. As an overall point of comparison, the last column in the table shows the mean difference between the 1987 and 1977 influence scores for each level (A, F, M-W, and M-R) for the sample as a whole. (Note that because of the way the relative influence measures were constructed, a negative score for M-W and M-R indicates that, compared to management, the influence of workers' and representative bodies increased between 1977 and 1987, while a positive score denotes a decrease in the relative influence of labour groups over time.)

The overall pattern of results is in line with the contingency argument from management strategy outlined above. In particular, the data show that in Type I organizations there was a general tendency for the absolute and relative influence of both workers and representative bodies to decline over the ten-year period under consideration, while in Type II and III organizations the change was in the opposite direction. As

TABLE 4.9. Changes in Influence (PO) Scores over Time (PO 1987–PO 1977) for Different Types of Scenario and for the Total Sample, by Level

	Scenarios			
	Type I Organizations	Type II Organizations	Type III Organizations	Total Sample
Mean 1987–1977 influence (PO) score for workers (A)	-0.18† (N=17)	0.10 (N=52)	0.52* (N=18)	0.14* (N=92)
Mean 1987–1977 Influence (PO) score for representative bodies (F)	-0.11 (N=11)	0.07 (N=59)	0.29* (N=16)	0.14* (N=91)
Mean 1987–1977 Relative influence (PO) score for management-workers (M-W)	0.06 (N=19)	-0.17* (N=53)	-0.32 (N=15)	-0.15* (N=92)
Mean 1987–1977 Relative influence (PO) score for management-representative bodies (M-R)	0.13 (N=12)	-0.13 (N=58)	-0.18* (N=16)	-0.14* (N=91)

Key:
Type I Scenario = High (above average) 1977 Influence Scores and High (above average) increases in unemployment rate between 1977 and 1987.
Type II Scenario = Either (a) High (above average) 1977 Influence Scores and low (below average) increases in unemployment between 1977 and 1987; or (b) Low (below average) 1977 Influence Scores and High (above average) increases in unemployment between 1977 and 1987.
Type III Scenario = Low (below average) 1977 Influence Scores and Low (below average) increases in unemployment between 1977 and 1987.
* = Difference between 1987 and 1977 Influence Scores across three types of scenarios is statistically significant (<.05 level).
† = Increase or decrease between 1987 and 1977 Influence Scores is statistically significant (<.05 level).
N = Number of organizations in category.

expected, moreover, the changes which took place in Type II systems, which account for a majority of the organizations in the sample, tended, in all cases, to be less marked than in Type III organizations. However, the table also shows that, except for workers, the differences in trends across the three types of organizations, although in the expected direction, are not statistically significant. This is not, perhaps, all that surprising given the aggregate nature of the analysis and the rather broad criteria which were used to categorize the organizations in the sample. What it does suggest, however, is that there are other factors, apart from those identified in the model, which helped to condition patterns of influence distribution in organizations between 1977 and 1987. This is reflected also in the results of the longitudinal regression analyses reported in Tables 4.7 and 4.8 above. Inspection of the adjusted R^2 figures shows that the management strategy model explains between 10 and 42 per cent of the variance in changes in patterns of labour influence between 1977 and 1987, depending on whether an additive or contingency version of the model is applied to the data.

In summary, the results of the descriptive analysis presented in Table 4.9 provide additional support for a 'management strategy' interpretation of the data. They also suggest that there are other specific factors, besides those identified in our model, which are likely to affect management's willingness and capacity to act within the enterprise. At the same time, though, the results of the regression analysis show that, taken together, the variables in our model account for an important proportion of the variance in changes in patterns of labour influence between 1977 and 1987. In particular, some of the more complex contingency hypotheses linked to the management strategy model find strong support in the data. Although in need of refinement, therefore, the analysis presented above goes some way in explaining changes in patterns of influence distribution in organizations after 1977 and, in the process, directs attention to important elements of both continuity and change in the position of labour groups within plant-level systems of industrial relations in the 1980s.

CONCLUSIONS

Earlier in this chapter, the determinants of patterns of influence distribution in organizations have been examined first through a cross-sectional and then through a longitudinal analysis of the 1977 and 1987 data. Here we shall limit ourselves to highlighting the most salient findings and conclusions to emerge from the chapter as a whole.

The first point to note concerns the lack of stability exhibited by some of our results. As we have seen, there are a number of differences between the results of the cross-sectional and longitudinal analyses. In terms of the results of the 1977 and 1987 cross-sectional analyses, the main difference is in relation to the contextual variables. None of these variables emerged as significant predictors of influence in 1987 even though a number of them, including various structural characteristics of the enterprise, were significant in 1977. Nor did any of these variables attain significance in the longitudinal analysis. More importantly, the cross-sectional and longitudinal analyses point to different conclusions concerning the determinants of patterns of influence in organizations. In particular, the longitudinal analysis failed to confirm the results of the two cross-sectional analyses concerning the importance of institutional norms as predictors of the overall distribution of influence in organizations. Instead, as we have seen, the longitudinal analysis suggests that the unemployment rate is a more important determinant of patterns of influence distribution than is the institutional framework for participation.

These differences between the results of the cross-sectional and longitudinal analyses cannot be readily explained, particularly since they may be due to a number of factors. They may, for example, be a function of country-specific effects, or of the quality of some of the 1977 and 1987 data, or of specific time-lag effects not captured in the cross-sectional data. A detailed exploration of these issues is beyond the scope of the present discussion, although the differences between the results of the two sets of analyses clearly merit closer investigation. The point to note here is that, in principle at least, causal relationships between variables are best explored through diachronic rather than synchronic forms of analysis, although the latter are clearly also important in understanding patterns of relationships between variables. In assessing the relative importance of different variables as predictors of influence, it may be better, therefore, to place greater emphasis on the results of the longitudinal rather than on those of the cross-sectional analysis without, however, disregarding the results of the latter.

On this basis, three main overall findings can be said to emerge from our analysis. First, our results suggest that patterns of influence distribution in organizations are not significantly conditioned by contextual factors. At best, contextual variables, including structural characteristics of the enterprise, such as technology, size, and sector, have only a marginal impact on the distribution of influence. Second, the results of the longitudinal analysis suggest that the relationship between patterns of *de jure* participation and the distribution of influence may be considerably more tenuous, and potentially also more complex, than was suggested in the original IDE I study. In view of the more positive results obtained in the two cross-sectional analyses in this respect, the explanatory role of institutional norms can by no means be discounted. On balance, however, it would appear that the institutional framework for participation is not as important a determinant of patterns of influence distribution in organizations as we originally thought.

The final point is linked specifically to the longitudinal analysis and has to do with our overall interpretation of the IDE data in terms of the management strategy argument. As we have seen, changes in the absolute and relative influence of workers and representative bodies at the plant between 1977 and 1987 were found to be related primarily to two factors, changes in the general state of the labour-market and the 'pre-existing' distribution of influence within the enterprise. Our results suggest, however, that the relationship between unemployment and influence is more complex than is usually assumed in the literature. In particular, our analysis suggests that changes in economic conditions do not automatically or inevitably lead to changes in the distribution of influence between management and labour within the enterprise. Whether or not changes in unemployment lead to changes in patterns of influence distribution depends, at least in part, on the particular context involved. In particular, it depends on the 'pre-existing' distribution of influence within the enterprise which, in turn, affects managerial strategies and behaviour within the organization. More specifically, our analysis suggests that the greatest deterioration in the position of labour groups between 1977 and 1987 tended to occur in plant level systems of industrial relations where in the 1970s labour used to exercise a relatively high degree of influence over organizational decisions, but where there subsequently was a sharp rise in unemployment in the 1980s. It is in organizations where labour was strongest in 1977, in fact, that management was most likely to want to try to take advantage of the changed economic conditions of the 1980s to reassert its control within the enterprise. In other words, our analysis suggests that the impact of economic variables on influence tends to be mediated by historical conditions and by management strategy. As such, it directs attention to important elements of both continuity and change in plant level systems of industrial relations between 1977 and 1987 depending on the particular combination of economic and historical conditions which happened to obtain in different organizations during this period.

5

Summary and Conclusions

OBJECTIVES

The present study had a number of objectives. The overall and primary aim was to look at the same organizations in the same countries in Europe and Israel ten years after the first survey, and learn about any changes that might have occurred. More specifically, we wanted to see whether the external and formal influence and power structures and the extent of participative behaviour inside organizations had changed and whether the previous finding of a positive relationship between formal power structures and *de facto* participation was still true in the 1980s.

The most ambitious and most difficult aim was to see whether a longitudinal link between the two cross-sectional studies might give us some insight into possible causal relationships over time. To do justice to this ambitious endeavour, we had to try and select a group of contingencies which could be hypothesized as strengthening or weakening the relationships between our major dimensions and, in addition, assess the impact of selected economic and technological changes (in particular the rate of unemployment) over the intervening period, up to 1987. Not all our aims could be accomplished. The downturn in economic conditions which affected our sample of companies also reduced the availability of research funding and, consequently, we had to be content with a less complete schema than we would have wanted to use. However, the replication study benefited from our analysis of the 1977 results, where we found that some aspects of the enquiry were relatively unimportant and could be dispensed with. At the same time, although we had to economize our resources, we wanted to introduce a few variables that had gained salience in the intervening years. Details of the research plan that emerged are described in Chapter 1 and the consequences of the tactical decisions that had to be made are discussed in the analyses contained in Chapters 3 and 4.

In this final chapter we will report selectively on a number of findings that are thought to have strategic relevance for future research as well as for industrial relations policy.

THE VALUE OF REPLICATION

In spite of the limitation of resources available to carry out the 1987 study, we are convinced that replication studies are of considerable scientific and practical value. We can, however, understand why the vast majority of industrial relations and organizational studies use a cross-sectional design without wishing that this state of affairs continues indefinitely or is considered adequate for scientific or policy purposes. A replication study with only two measurement points may not be as interesting as one that has three, or even more, and for the purpose of understanding behavioural dynamics, longitudinal studies have to use methods of tracing structural, social, and psychological processes over prolonged periods of time (Heller 1984).

Nevertheless, the results from the present replication study show very clearly that, while some findings from 1977 were confirmed and can consequently be considered more secure, other conclusions have to be modified in the light of the evidence from an analysis of the available 1977–87 data. This possibility undoubtedly enriches our understanding of the interaction between aspects of organizational behaviour and the economic-political environment. We were also fortunate that after such a long interval of time the majority of researchers who had taken part in the earlier study were still available to carry out the second study, and that most of the companies had survived and agreed to work with us again.

While a decade is always a long time in an organization's life, the period 1977–1987 was in some respects unusually turbulent. It included a major oil crisis which precipitated a significant downturn in economic activity, an increase in competition—particularly from Japan—and a noticeable increase in unemployment, which affected all countries in our sample, but some much more severely than others. In addition, the decade was characterized by very substantial changes in technology in manufacturing as well as in service industries.

In most countries the political balance had moved to the right, attitudes towards trade unions had become less favourable, and the role of employer was more dominant. These and other factors have, of course, varied somewhat from country to country. In order to obtain the necessary background information against which to evaluate specific country results, the reader is referred to Chapter 2.

OUTLINE OF THE STUDIES

The principal focus of both research studies was the distribution of influence at all levels of organization, its antecedents, and consequences. Both studies were based on an examination of sixteen decisions, covering short-term operational, mainly shop-floor issues, as well as longer-term strategic decisions. The respondents were key senior management and trade union personnel within each of the Seventy-two companies that were involved in 1977 as well as 1987. The replication study included ten out of the original twelve countries: Belgium, Denmark, Finland, Germany, Britain, Israel, Netherlands, Norway, Sweden, and Yugoslavia. In addition, the 1987 study included Poland and Japan.

In each organization, respondents were interviewed and filled in a number of questionnaires. The answers to the set of standardized sixteen decisions covered an influence distribution continuum on a scale 1 (no influence), 2 (little influence), 3 (moderate influence), 4 (much influence), 5 (very much influence). This distribution of Influence (abbreviated PO) was assessed for all levels of the organization (worker, first-line supervisor, middle management, top management, and representative bodies: works' councils or joint consultative committees plus some which will not be reviewed here).

The major antecedent variable was Participative Structure. This was a measure of formal prescribed participation based on laws or recognized collective agreements, measured on a scale from 1 to 6.

FINDINGS FROM COUNTRY DATA

The overall pattern and distribution of Influence in the seventy-two organizations from ten countries did not change very much over the decade. Some changes in influence at the lowest level of organization were found in four countries. Worker-influence increased slightly in Israel, Sweden, and Finland, but declined in Yugoslavia.

There were more substantial changes for Representative Bodies. In Britain and Yugoslavia their influence declined, while in other countries, particularly in Israel and Sweden, and to a lesser extent in Finland, it increased.

At the level of top management, the Influence scores (PO) between 1977 and 1987 were identical for Yugoslavia and Finland. They declined very slightly in Belgium, Britain, Denmark, Netherlands, Norway, and Sweden, and increased slightly in Israel. In Germany the drop in top management influence was fairly large (see Fig. 3.15).

The changes in formal Participative Structures over the same period showed substantially more variability. Most movements were in an upward direction (see Table 5.1). Participative Structures supporting senior management registered consistent increases in every country except Britain, where it declined slightly. The increase was very large for Israel; substantial for Denmark and Norway; moderate in the Netherlands, Sweden, and Finland; and small in Yugoslavia.

At the lowest level of organization, there were increases in formal Participative Structures in Britain, the Netherlands, Israel, Norway, and

Finland. In Yugoslavia and Belgium, this support declined and there was no change in Denmark and Germany.

An important objective of the present research is to test the assumption, derived from the 1977 study, that Participative Structures could have a determining influence on participative behaviour at the lowest level of organization measured by our Influence-Power-Continuum. It is therefore interesting to look at the difference in Participative Structure scores between top management and workers over the ten-year period (see Table 3.2). This difference has increased in six out of the ten countries (Belgium, Denmark, Israel, Norway, Sweden, Yugoslavia), most noticeably in Belgium and Norway. In four countries the difference has decreased (Germany, Britain, Netherlands, and Finland).

If we examine the changes in Participative Structures and *de facto* participation over the ten years, country by country, we find no consistent relationship in the pattern of changes (see Table 5.1). Two explanations may spring to mind. One is that Participative Structures do not determine the amount of Influence available at the level of workers. Alternatively, it is possible that changes in formal Participative Structures take a long time to work through the system and affect shop-floor behaviour. Our data do not tell us when in the decade 1977–87 the structural changes took place. If, for instance, many of the changes took place in the mid-1980s, then one would not expect the consequences to have cascaded down to behavioural changes at the lowest level of organization by 1987. In other words, there may have been a time-lag in the system.

The highest level of prescribed formal Influence is, in each country, given to senior management, except in Britain (see Fig. 3.4). Britain is

TABLE 5.1. *Changes over the Decade 1977–1987 in Participative Structures (PS) and de facto Influence (PO) for Workers and Top management*

	Worker level		Top management	
	PS	PO	PS	PO
Belgium	−	+	+	−
Denmark	0	+	++	−
Germany	0	0	+	−−
Britain	+	0	−	−
Netherlands	+	0	+	−
Israel	+	+	++	+
Norway	+	−	++	−
Sweden	0	+	+	−
Yugoslavia	−	−	+	0
Finland	+	−	+	0

Key: − = less; + = more; ++ = much more; 0 = unchanged

unusual in this sample for having very few well-defined formal or legal rules relating to participation. Nevertheless the *de facto* power of senior management in Britain is substantial and about the same as in other countries. From another project which followed up the 1977 Industrial Democracy research, we also know that in addition to externally prescribed formal Structures, there are company-level prescribed or sanctioned norms (which we call Status Power) that have a strong determining influence on the *de facto* distribution of influence (DIO 1979).

FINDINGS FROM COUNTRY DATA

We now come to report on the more global analysis for which country data is aggregated, in order to explore the extent to which patterns of *de facto* Influence distribution are affected by formal Power Structures. The calculations were carried out separately for the 1987 data, as well as for the strictly comparable variables from 1977. Finally, a longitudinal analysis was carried out to trace the relationship of formal Power Structures on the distribution of *de facto* influence between 1977 and 1987. The only macro-economic factor in these analyses is the annual average percentage of unemployment 1985–7 and 1975–7.

This detailed work is described in Chapter 4, but only the more important policy relevant conclusions are reported here.

To make the two time-periods comparable, it was necessary to re-analyse the 1977 data by leaving out variables not covered in 1987 and removing France and Italy because they did not take part in the replication (largely because of the unavailability of research funding).

This new 1977 analysis reconfirmed the earlier conclusion that formal Power Structures predict the overall Influence distribution between management and labour. This prediction was particularly strong for the impact of Power Structures on the Influence of Representative Bodies.

A high rate of unemployment is usually assumed to reduce the influence of labour and this was confirmed for nine countries. However, it is of some interest to report that, under certain circumstances, a high degree of unemployment does not have this negative effect on workers, which in fact was the case with Yugoslavia. It is very likely that the robustness of that participative system was a function of its having been very firmly embedded in the socio-political system at that time. (Warner 1989).

If we leave Yugoslavia out of the 1977 re-analysis, unemployment is a stronger predictor of Worker Influence than formal Power Structures. Workers in the service sector have more influence than in manufacturing, but other contingency factors, like size of organization or product complexity, made no impact.

The 1977 statistical analysis provides a fairly clear picture of the *de facto* influence of top managers and worker representative bodies. In both cases, the impact of formal Power Structures and unemployment are strong predictors. In the case of Representative Bodies, the unemployment rate has a negative effect, but in predicting the Influence of top managers, it has a positive effect.

Analysis of the 1987 data has to be approached with caution, for reasons explained in Chapter 4, but a number of conclusions and comparisons with 1977 can be made. In spite of the substantial economic and social changes over the decade separating the two measurement periods, there are important similarities in the overall results. In particular, the apparently causal impact of formal Participative Structures on the pattern of Influence for Workers and Representative Bodies is repeated in 1987. In both time-periods, we can observe a similar prediction between Participative Structures and the difference in the extent of Influence between top management and labour. Unemployment strengthens the position of management in 1977 as well as, more weakly, in 1987. Unemployment weakened the influence of labour in 1977 and, to a lesser extent, also in 1987.

FINDINGS FROM LONGITUDINAL ANALYSIS

Thus far we have confined ourselves to a somewhat static analysis of the results of the two periods of research and a comparison between them. Finally, it is important to make use of the longitudinal data in an attempt to introduce a dynamic pattern of relationships into the discussion of industrial relations over the decade 1977–87. This was achieved by combining the statistics from the two periods and conducting various analyses with this new two-period data set.

One objective was to see whether the pattern of Influence at the end of the decade was conditioned by factors derived from the material collected ten years previously. Furthermore, the two-period data could also be used to study changes in patterns of Influence Distribution between 1977 and 1987 and related to three factors:

  (i) changes in formal Participative Structures (PS);
 (ii) changes in the general rate of unemployment over the decade; and
(iii) the extent to which different groups in the organizations exercised Influence (PO) at the beginning of the decade in 1977.

The procedures for carrying out these analyses are complex and again we will only report the most important, policy-relevant findings.

Perhaps the most important result of the longitudinal analysis is to demonstrate that it leads, in one or two important respects, to different conclusions from the cross-sectional analysis. In particular, it shows that formal Participative Structures are less important predictors for the pattern of Influence distribution than the indices of unemployment. This conclusion substantially amends the conclusion derived from the 1977 study alone (IDE 1981*b*). It is, of course, important to bear in mind that the 1977–87 period was fairly exceptionally turbulent, in that it combined a major oil price-generated economic recession with substantially increased economic competition and changes in technological sophistication. One consequence of these indicators of turbulence was the increase of unemployment in each of the ten countries. It would be important to repeat such a longitudinal analysis during a less turbulent decade, when the impact of Participative Structures on the *de facto* distribution of Influence may very well turn out to be dominant. An important refinement was introduced into the longitudinal analysis by testing two alternative models of accounting for changing patterns of influence between the different organizational groups over time. A system 'Inertia model' would predict that groups that were powerful in 1977 would be able to survive well even under unfavourable conditions, while groups that started off weakly would lose ground. An alternative 'Management Strategy Model' assumes that during a recession, management would actively seek to reduce the power of the influential groups which could appear to threaten the managerial prerogative, while they would not be concerned to take steps against weaker groups.

In both models, the strategy would also have to take account of changes in the rate of unemployment and the strength of Participative Structures.

The statistical analysis strongly supports the Management Strategy Model. Over the ten-year period, labour tended to lose ground in organizations where it had been strong in the 1970s, rather than where it started off without posing a threat to management. The management strategy of reducing the strength of labour which it might have seen as a threat to its own position, was facilitated in places where unemployment was high.

Where unemployment was not high and labour was not particularly strong in the 1977 research, the Influence of workers did not change very much. In these circumstances it is quite likely that management initiated quasi-participative human resources measures, like briefing groups and various employee involvement programmes, including quality circles (Guest and Peccei 1992).

INTERPRETATION AND DISCUSSION

The arguments in favour of measures to support organizational democracy or in opposition to it have been prominent over several decades. In the United States, the argument in favour of participation of employees is sometimes advocated as a way of increasing the competitiveness of American industry *vis-à-vis* Japan (Cole 1979; Lawler 1986: 10). In Europe the arguments against participation by some managements, particularly in Britain, are the reverse: namely, that companies would lose competitiveness. However, in general, the debate in Europe is conducted as much on the political as on the economic level (Foundation for the Improvement of Living and Working Conditions 1989).

The academic and research literature is very extensive (see, for instance, the series of Yearbooks and Handbooks: Crouch and Heller 1979; Wilpert and Sorge 1984; Stern and McCarthy 1986; Lammers and Szell 1989; Russell and Rus 1991).

There is no agreement about what increases in organizational democracy should achieve (Wagner and Gooding 1987). Employers and some academics would like to see increases in profitability or a reduction of conflict, while political scientists see organizational democracy as a twentieth-century extension of political democracy and therefore as something worth while in itself. Some trade unions are concerned that through co-optation, successful participative practices would undermine the power of collective bargaining and managers are concerned that organizational democracy will usurp their right to manage.

Against the background of these controversies, our research produces some useful evidence, which is relevant for the formulation of policy. To begin with, the research in the ten countries separated by ten years shows that, on average, neither *de jure* Participative Structures nor de *facto* Participative Behaviour are very highly developed in the majority of our countries or organizations. Looking at Table 3.4. giving 1987 data, one can see that on our 5-point Influence and Power Continuum, the highest score for workers is 2.44 for Yugoslavia. This signifies a position half-way between 'little' and 'moderate' influence. Most scores are much closer to 'little influence' and six are between 'no influence' and 'little influence'.

Is this amount of influence-sharing a matter of concern? Could this evidence give objective support to management's fear of usurpation or trade unions' anxiety of weakening an adversarial policy? Furthermore, given such a very low level of participation, even in Germany where legally supported co-determination has existed since the early 1950s, is it reasonable to expect participation to produce measurable improvement in an organization's profitability or a reduction in conflict? Of course, the figures we cite are averages and they probably exclude the well-known leaders in the field of organizational democracy.

The figure for the Influence of Representative Bodies, for example, is higher; in Yugoslavia it reaches 3.44, that is to say, half-way between 'moderate' and 'much' influence, but in Germany, with its forty-year tradition of works councils, it is only 2.69 (between 'little' and 'moderate' influence).

The formal, often legal Prescription to induce participative behaviour shows a wide variation between countries. The 1987 data (Table 3.1) gives the Representative Bodies in Yugoslavia an average score of 4.79 (on a 6-point scale). This result signifies that they are close to achieving joint decision-making rights with management. In the case of Germany, with 3.99, it almost reaches the obligatory right of a group to be consulted before a decision is taken. The legal prescription for Poland almost reaches such a position, but in Japan, Finland, and Britain, the formal structures fail to provide even the right to receive information. This finding of the very low average level of *de facto* participation and the moderate but very varying formal supportive structures must be borne in mind when drawing policy relevant conclusions about the current and future role of participative behaviour in organizations.

The Commission of the European Communities has tried to achieve a common policy on information-sharing and consultative rights since 1972, but progress has been very slow in the face of heavy opposition from management. The original proposals, which were based on the German system, have been very considerably scaled down. One of the practical problems facing the European Commission, is the great variety of Participative Structures and practices in its member countries.

Our finding that there are very few contingencies that affect the relationship between Participative Structures and Influence Sharing behaviour may turn out to be a useful support in the formulation of national or cross-national policies. In 1977 as well as in 1987, factors like size of organization, level of automation, skill requirements, product complexity, perceived market dominance, and political instability were of little significance in understanding the dynamics of participative behaviour. This result would suggest that a single framework of requirements within a European Company Law structure could be applied to information-disclosure and participation in organizations of different sizes (though our sample extends only from 100 to 2,000 employees), skill requirements, etc.

Similar considerations apply to policy at the level of organizations. Findings in support of the 'Management Strategy Model' suggest that under the umbrella of an economic recession and high unemployment, companies may have deliberately reduced the influence of labour where it had previously been relatively strong (Chapter 4). It is possible that such a strategy was based on an emotional rather than a factual interpretation of the strength of labour's real influence in the decision-making process. In support of this is the finding from the 1977 research that when respondents are asked how much influence they would like to have, compared to what they currently have, the increase is very moderate (IDE 1981*b*: 191–4). Other research has reported similar findings (Wall and Lischeron 1977).

In looking at the overall result of the longitudinal replication study reported here, it is reassuring that over a turbulent ten-year period, the basic pattern of results shows substantial stability.

It would seem that some formal prescriptive or legally supported Participative Structures lend support to participative behaviour reaching down to the lowest level of organization. The very high unemployment rate in the decade 1977–87 undoubtedly made its own major impact on reducing the influence of labour during this period, and it is therefore necessary to look at these relationships again during a less turbulent decade. It would also be important to explore the length of time it takes in the different countries for structures to affect behaviour.

In this connection, it is worth reporting briefly on a longitudinal research following the 1977 field-work. Three countries from the Industrial Democracy in Europe team (IDE 1981*b*) were able to carry out a five-year in-depth study in seven organizations using the same Influence-Power measuring instruments, but adding several output measures and refinements which can only be tackled in a continuous monitoring type of longitudinal research. The study, called 'Decisions in Organizations', took place in Britain, the Netherlands, and Yugoslavia (DIO 1979; Heller *et al.* 1988).

Several findings from the DIO research are relevant for the replication study. In the first place, once again the overall distribution of Influence over the different levels of organization was similar to the results reported here and did not differ significantly over the five years of the research. The DIO study followed 217 tactical and strategic decisions from start-up to implementation. Instead of measuring formal Participative Structures at the national level, it used a structural measure called Status Power (SP), which assessed the formal authority of each group or committee in each organization. The measure was based on written evidence or long-established policy. The predictive potential of Status Power on *de facto* participation of top management and workers was very substantial and significant.

This finding reinforces the evidence on the importance of structures in the decision-making processes of the 1977–87 replication study. Taken together with the DIO results, it seems that a reasonable amount of Influence Distribution (PO), down to the lowest level of organization, probably requires formal structural support, either at the national or organizational level, or at both. It has important policy implications and weakens the argument in favour of voluntaristic *ad hoc* arrangements in support of participation. It may also add to our knowledge of organizational behaviour by emphasizing the importance of formal structures as a key variable in attempting not only internal but also societal change.

We may also generalize these findings with respect to predicting longitudinal shifts in behaviour over time and the difficulties in achieving this.

Appendix A
Regression Analyses

TABLE A1. *Re-analysis of 1977 Data excluding Yugoslavia: Regressions of Influence (PO 1977) on to other Variables (1977) for short-term Decisions (Cluster 2), by Level*

Predictors (1977 values)	Regression Equations (A to M-R)						
	A Influence workers	B Influence supervisors	C Influence middle management	D Influence top management	F Influence representative bodies	M-W Influence management-workers	M-R Influence management-representatives
PS score per level (A to M-R)	–			–	0.50	+	0.31
Unemployment rate	– 0.40*	– 0.28	+	0.41	– 0.21	0.46	0.28
Formal independence		+	+				
Market dominance						–	–
Political instability sector	0.33		0.29			–	+
Skill requirements				–	–		
Product complexity				0.48			
Functional difference				– 0.27			
Vertical span				– 0.26	– 0.45		
Formalization							– 0.22
Adjusted R²	0.24	0.16	0.05	0.38	0.24	0.23	0.17
(N)	(82)	(76)	(75)	(63)	(78)	(80)	(78)

Key:
Same as in Table 4.1 except that all influence (PO) and *de jure* participation (PS) scores used in the regression equations (A to M-R) refer to the subset of short-term discussions (Cluster 2) covered in the research rather than to the total set of 16 decisions.

* Numbers in the table are standardized regression coefficients.

TABLE A2. *Re-analysis of 1977 Data excluding Yugoslavia: Regressions of Influence (PO 1977) on to other Variables (1977) for Medium-term Decisions (Decisions Cluster 3), by Level*

Predictors (1977 values)	Regression Equations (A to M-R)						
	A Influence workers	B Influence supervisors	C Influence middle management	D Influence top management	F Influence representative bodies	M-W Influence management-workers	M-R Influence management-representatives
PS score per level (A to M-R)	0.26*	+	+	+	0.67	0.29	0.45
Unemployment rate	–	+	+	0.29	–0.23	0.31	0.35
Market dominance					+	0.25	–
Political instability sector		–0.26					
Level automation			0.24				
Product complexity	0.22						
Formalization					+	–0.19	–0.27
Adjusted R^2	0.15	0.03	0.05	0.12	0.50	0.27	0.33
(N)	(82)	(77)	(72)	(75)	(78)	(80)	(78)

Key:

Same as in Table 4.1 except that all influence (PO) and *de jure* in participation (PS) scores used in the regression equations (A to M-R) refer to the subset of medium-term decisions (Cluster 3) covered in the research rather than to the total set of 16 decisions.

* Numbers in the table are standardized regression coefficients.

TABLE A3. *Re-analysis of 1977 Data excluding Yugoslavia: Regressions of Influence (PO 1977) on to other Variables (1987) for Long-term Decisions (Cluster 4), by Level*

	Regression Equations (A to M-R)						
Predictors (1977 values)	A Influence workers	B Influence supervisors	C Influence middle management	D Influence top management	F Influence representative bodies	M-W Influence management-workers	M-R Influence management-representatives
PS score per level (A to M-R)	–	–	–	+	+	0.21	0.27
Unemployment rate	–	–	–	0.23	–0.27	+	+
Formal independence		0.25*	0.37	0.30		0.31	
Political instability					+	–	+
Functional difference	+			–0.36	+		
Vertical span			–0.26				
Formalization		–0.39		–0.43		–0.46	–0.21
Adjusted R²	0.02	0.18	0.17	0.38	0.09	0.31	0.13
(N)	(78)	(77)	(62)	(72)	(74)	(81)	(78)

Key:
Same as in Table 4.1 except that all influence (PO) and *de jure* participation (PS) scores used in the regression equations (A to M-R) refer to the subset of long-term decisions (Cluster 4) covered in the research rather than to the total set of 16 decisions.

* Numbers in the table are standardized regression coefficients.

TABLE A4. *Analysis of 1987 Data: Regressions of Influence (PO 1987) on to other Variables (1987) for Short-term Decisions (Cluster 2), by Level*

Predictors (1987 values)	Regression Equations (A to M-R)						
	A Influence workers	B Influence supervisors	C Influence middle management	D Influence top management	F Influence representative bodies	M-W Influence management-workers	M-R Influence management-representatives
PS score per level (A to M-R)	+	−	+	+	0.41	+	+
Unemployment rate	−	−	−	0.35	+	0.28	+
Formal independence		+				−	
Market dominance					−		
Political instability					+		
Functional difference					0.28		− 0.40
% Skilled		0.27*					
Adjusted R²	0.07	0.06	0.08	0.08	0.27	0.09	0.16
(N)	(66)	(58)	(88)	(66)	(61)	(66)	(61)

Key:
Same as in Table 4.1 except that all influence (PO) and *de jure* participation (PS) scores used in the regression equations (A to M-R) refer to the subset of short-term decisions (Cluster 2) covered in the research rather than to the total set of 16 decisions.

* Numbers in the table are standardized regression coefficients.

TABLE A5. *Analysis of 1987 Data: Regressions of Influence (PO 1987) on to other Variables (1987) for Medium-term Decisions (Cluster 3), by Level*

Predictors (1987 values)	Regression Equations (A to M-R)						
	A Influence workers	B Influence supervisors	C Influence middle management	D Influence top management	F Influence representative bodies	M-W Influence management-workers	M-R Influence management-representatives
PS score per level (A to M-R)	0.57*	+	+	+	0.62	+	0.50
Unemployment rate	+	+	−	+	+	+	+
Market dominance	− 0.22	−				+	
Level automation							
Product complexity		+	+				
Functional difference					+		− 0.30
Vertical Span				−			
Adjusted R²	0.37	0.03	0	0.05	0.40	0.03	0.33
(N)	(66)	(65)	(64)	(62)	(61)	(66)	(61)

Key:
Same as in Table 4.1 except that all influence (PO) and *de jure* participation (PS) scores used in the regression equations (A to M-R refer to the subset of medium-term decision (Cluster 3) covered in the research rather than to the total set of 16 decisions.

* Numbers in the table are standardized regression coefficients.

TABLE A6. *Analysis of 1987 Data: Regressions of Influence (PO 1987) on to other Variables (1987) for Long-term Decisions (Cluster 4), by Level*

Predictors (1987 values)	Regression Equations (A to M-R)						
	A Influence workers	B Influence supervisors	C Influence middle management	D Influence top management	F Influence representative bodies	M-W Influence management-workers	M-R Influence management-representatives
PS score per level (A to M-R)	0.53*	+	+	0.35	0.60	0.25	0.42
Unemployment rate	+	−	−	+	+	−	−
Market dominance		−					
Sector				−			
Level automation						0.26	
Product complexity	+						
Functional difference							−0.34
Formalization		+			+		
% Skilled		0.24	+				
Adjusted R^2	0.23	0.19	0.04	0.13	0.38	0.11	0.24
(N)	(66)	(56)	(56)	(90)	(61)	(65)	(60)

Key:
Same as in Table 4.1 except that all influence (PO) and *de jure* participation (PS) scores used in the regression equations (A to M-R) refer to the subset of long-term decisions (Cluster 4) covered in the research rather than to the total set of 16 decisions.

* Numbers in the table are standardized regression coefficients.

Tests of Robustness of 1987 Results

TABLE B1. *Analysis of 1987 Data: Regressions of Influence (PO 1987) on to other Variables (1987) for Total Decision Set by Level*

Predictors (1987)	Regression Equations (A to M-R)						
	A Influence workers	B Influence supervisors	C Influence middle management	D Influence top management	F Influence representative bodies	M-W Influence management-workers	M-R Influence management-representatives
(a) With contextual variables as predictors (same as Table 4.3)							
PS score per level (A to M-R)	0.50*				0.60	0.25	0.44
Unemployment rate	–	–	–	0.32	+	+	+
Formal independence	+		–	+		–	
Still requirements		–					
Product complexity	+		+				
Functional difference			+		+		–0.33
Adjusted R^2	0.25	0.03	0	0.07	0.41	0.09	0.29
(N)	(66)	(65)	(64)	(66)	(51)	(66)	(61)
(b) Without contextual variables as predictors – Full Sample							
PS score per level (A to M-R)	0.37*			+	0.60	+	0.56
Unemployment rate	–0.24	–	+	0.35	–	0.39	0.28
Adjusted R^2	0.20	0	0.01	0.10	0	0.10	0.33
(N)	(87)	(90)	(88)	(90)	(86)	(87)	(86)

TABLE B1. (contd.)

	Regression Equations (A to M-R)						
Predictors (1987)	A Influence workers	B Influence supervisors	C Influence middle management	D Influence top management	F Influence representative bodies	M-W Influence management-workers	M-R Influence management-representatives

(c) Without contextual variables as predictors but including only organizations covered in (a) above (i.e., subset of organizations for which 1987 data are available on the contextual variables)

	A	B	C	D	F	M-W	M-R
PS score per level (A to M-R)	0.51*	–	–	+	0.66	0.28	0.45
Unemployment rate	–	–	–	0.32	+	0.28	+
Adjusted R^2	0.26	0	0	0.09	0.39	0.10	0.19
(N)	(66)	(65)	(64)	(66)	(61)	(66)	(61)

* Numbers in table are standardized regression coefficients

Appendix C
Questionnaire List of IDE Publications

Personal Information Form (PIF)   Form 1

Notes and Instructions

For everybody who fills out PO1:

1. Management or management designate
2. Representative persons

plus the respondent for Top Management Interview (TOP-CON)

CODE
Country:
Sector:
Size:
Company # :
Person # :

Here are a number of questions about your background. It is understood that your information will be kept strictly confidential by the investigators. Please answer carefully.

1 [1.]*   **What is your *main* JOB FUNCTION?**
Enter the appropriate number in the box provided.
  (1) production (in manufacturing or service industry)
  (2) administration, personnel, general
       non-specialized management
  (3) technical, like: research and development,
       industrial engineering, quality control,
       operations research, work study, etc.
  (4) sales, marketing, purchasing, stores, etc.
  (5) finance, accounting
  (6) full-time employee representative

2 [2.]   **Give your JOB TITLE:**
To which of the four levels do you belong?
Enter the appropriate number in the box provided.**
  (1) Top or senior management (within two levels of
       the chief executive)
  (2) Middle management

(3) Supervisor (usually first level)
(4) Shop floor □

---

3 [6.] How long have you been with the company?
(In years. If less than one year put 'Less'. Include
members or change of name of company, etc.) □

---

4 [7.] Level of EDUCATION completed
(Enter appropriate number in box.)

(1) Primary education
(2) Secondary education
(3) Higher education excluding university
(4) University degree or equivalent

**5 [10.] Are you a member of a union or similar,
professional body?**   □ yes □ no

---

6   Are you an employee representative?   □ yes □ no

---

*   Numbers in brackets: original question number
** As not all firms will have a differentiated hierarchy according to these
categories, take as top management those who are considered to be at the top
of the firm.

Notes and Instructions

This questionnaire is to be answered by key respondents, minimum of two:

1. Management or management designate
2. Key person from side of employee representatives

CODE
Country:
Sector:
Size:
Company # :
Person # :

Decision List PO1$_1$

1. **Improvements in work conditions of a work group on the workers' level** (dust, noise, safety)
2. **Appointment of a new department head**
3. **Establishment of criteria and procedures for hiring and selection of new employees**
4. **Whether workers can follow a vocational training course** (during work hours)
5. **Permanent transfer of workers to other jobs within the plant**
6. **Major capital investment, e.g. an additional production line, a new plant, etc.**
7. **Whether the company should make a completely new product**
8. **To establish who will be the immediate superior on the workers' level**
9. **Changes in how much a certain grade** (wage group) **shall earn** (beyond possible existing collective bargaining agreements)
10. **Replacement of personal equipment** (hand tools) **of workers** (not trivial things like pencils, etc.)
11. **Change in the way one or more departments are organized**
12. **Assignment of tasks to workers**
13. **Dismissal of one of the workers**
14. **Whether or not work study technique is to be used** (e.g. stopwatch, time-and-motion studies)

15. **The timing of a worker's holiday** (for periods outside possible establishment holidays)
16. **From when to when working hours are** (flexible ends of working hours)
17. **Introduction of large-scale technology in the firm** (to be specified in the context of the given firm)
18. **Substantial dismissal of work force in the firm** (at least 5–10%)

§1 Influence on decisions

> **Instruction**
>
> Add issues from Decision list $PO1_1$ and have respondent answer for each group's influence on each decision

1   **How much influence do the different groups have over each decision?**

	No influence	Little influence	Moderate influence	Much influence	Very much influence
A Workers					
B First line supervisors					
C Middle management					
D Top management					
E Level above plant					
F Internal repr. bodies					
G External groups					

2   **Is the decision usually reached through disagreement?**
(No = 1; Yes = 2; Don't know = 3)

Decision no.	1	2	3	4	5	6	7	8	9
Response									
Decision no.	10	11	12	13	14	15	16	17	18
Response									

§2 Technological impact

Here again our decision areas. To what extent has technological change in your firm during the last ten years had an impact on each of these areas:

	No impact	Little impact	Moderate impact	Much impact	Major impact
1. Improvements in work conditions of your work group (dust, noise, safety)					
2. Appointment of a new department head					

Instruction

Add all other decisions up to #18. see $PO1_1$ decision

§3 Introduction phases involvement

Major technical changes usually comprise several critical steps:

1. The decision whether or not to introduce a new technology
2. The consideration of different alternatives
3. The choice of what kind of specific technology to introduce
4. The decision of how to go about implementing the new technology

With respect to the *major technological changes* in your firm during the last ten years:

How were the different groups *involved* in the different phases?

....

1   **In the phase whether or not to introduce the new technology the different groups were involved** (tick each group):

Involvement

Groups	they are not involved at all	they were informed before-hand	they could give opinion	they participated with equal weight	they could decide on their own
A Workers					
B First line supervisors					
C Middle management					
D Top management					
E Level above plant					
F Internal repr. Body					
G External groups (e.g. banks, unions; Specify: . . . .)					

....

2   **In the phase of considering different alternatives**

Instruction
Same as above

....

3   **In the phase of *choosing the specific kind* of technology to be introduced**

Instruction
Same as above

....

4   **In the phase of implementing the new technology**

Instruction
Same as above

....

§4 Resistance Possibility (PO4)

1 **With respect to significant technological changes in your firm, to what extent could below mentioned groups resist a decision:**

	They can not resist at all	They can delay but not change	They can change to some extent	They can change to a large extent	They can completely stop implementation of decision
A Workers					
B Formen					
C Middle management					
D Top management					
E Bodies above this organization					
F Work council					
G External bodies					

2 **With respect to a decision on *substantial dismissal* of the work force** (5–10%)

> **Instruction**
>
> Same as above

§5 Training and labor market

1 **Has over the period of the past 10 years the need of training of your employees in your firm (in order to meet the skill requirements)**

increased   3

remained the same   2

lessened   1

If 3 : in what fields? . . . .

Appendix C

2 **How easy or difficult is it to find an equivalent job** (in terms of pay and competence level) **in this area for a**

	very easy	easy	difficult	very difficult
skilled worker				
semi-skilled worker				
unskilled worker				

Contextual Characteristics—(CON)   Form 3

CODE
Country:
Sector:
Size:
Company # :
Person # :

Notes and Instructions

With this form we would like to collect some information on the main characteristics of this firm within its industrial setting. The questionnaire is the basis for a personal interview of the researcher with a knowledgeable key person in the organization. This may be a member of the top management or someone designated by the top management.

Structure of Questionnaire

1. Technology
2. Organizational Structure
3. Personnel Policy
4. Economic Data
5. Top Management Interview Guide

Notes

Respondents will usually be members or designates of the top management. If other specialists are appointed for particular parts, make sure that at least questionnaire part No. 5 is answered by a member of the top management.

- look upon this questionnaire as a guideline and apply it creatively

- ask questions as open questions, probe for explanations, data and further information, and only at the end of the discussion tick one of the boxes, preferably jointly with the respondent.

- explain our concepts and ask for the actual usage and specifics of terms, classifications etc., discuss comparibility of classifications and terminology

- the original numbering has been kept in this questionnaire although the questions have been reordered and in some cases amended

- coding conventions:

  not applicable = 9 ⎫ in all columns of the
  no answer   = 8 ⎬ respective variable
  don't know   = 7 ⎭

  example: 2.13.2. vertical span

Appendix C

$$\text{don't know} = \frac{38}{\;} \left| \frac{39}{7} \right| \frac{40}{7} \left| \frac{41}{7} \right| \frac{42}{7}$$

- in case you encounter problems of translation refer to the original Aston-questionnaires published in:
  - (a) Pugh, Hickson, Hinings, and Turner, 'Dimensions of Organization Structure', *ASQ* (1968)
  - (b) Pugh and Hickson, *Organizational Structure in its Context*, The Aston Programme 1, Heath (1976)
- a synopsis of concepts is attached as Appendix 3
- we have renumbered the questions sequentially and have put old numbering in brackets

§1 Technology

1 [1.1.a] Would you give a technical description of the product(s) or service(s) of this plant? 100

 - to which market(s) do you sell it? 101
 - how is it used by customers? (open question) 102
 - see product complexity scale, Appendix 1

---

2 [1.9.a] Multiplicity of outputs (circle) 103

Single output with standard variations	1
Single output with variations to costumer specification	2
Two or more outputs	3

---

3 [5.2] Would you describe the production/service flow of this plant? (Try to establish a flow chart and comment on it.) (Open question) 105

 - see work-flow complexity scale, Appendix 2

---

4 [1.2] In order to describe the level of technical complexity, we would like to know the type of machinery *most typical* of this plant, i.e. the most widely used in this plant and/or operated by the largest number of workers. 106

Scale for metal industry

Hand tools and manual machines	1
Powered machines and tools	2
Single-cycle automatics and self-feeding machines	3
Automatic: repeats cycle	4
Self-measuring and adjusting: feedback, or entirely computer controlled	5

Scale for service industry

Manual registers	1
Off-line computer files	3
Computer terminals for retrieval	4
Information fed and retrieved via computer terminals	5

---

5 [1.6] What is the level of automatically of the most automated pieces of equipment? 107

*these are variable numbers

Scale for metal industry

Hand tools and manual machines	1
Powered machines and tools	2
Single-cycle automatics and self-feeding machines	3
Automatic: repeats cycle	4
Self-measuring and adjusting: feed-back or entirely computer controlled	5

Scales for service industry

Manual registers	1
Mechanical and microfilm registers	2
Off-line computer files	3
Computer terminals for retrieval	4
Information fed and retrieved via computer terminals	5

---

6 [1.4] How much knowledge of the raw material, work flow, and products can be assumed for most (> 60%) of the workers?   108

(1) So much is known about the objects transformed that employees can approach nearly all non-routine problems:

(2) Enough is known about the raw material, or objects transformed so that the average employee can resolve many exceptions:

(3) Something is known about the objects transformed which enables employees to resolve some non-routine problems:

(4) A little is known about the raw material so that employees can resolve a *few* exceptional cases:

(5) So little is known about the objects transformed that employees cannot be expected to approach any non-routine cases

fill in the appropriate number ☐

---

7 [1.5] In case a crucial piece of machinery breaks down, how long will it take before this creates a critical situation for the output (delivery problems, etc.)?   109

Immediately (= 1 day)	1
Within 3 days	2
Within a week	3
Longer than a week/not severely	4

---

8 [1.8] How specific is the quality control? 110

Personal evaluation; rule of thumb	1
Partial and/or sample control	2
Specific and every single piece	3

9   The (rate of) **technological change(s) in this firm over the last ten years was/were**

very drastic (rapid)	5
—	4
—	3
—	2
—	1
no technological changes at all	0

§2. Organizational structure

10 [2.0] Ask for an organization chart and discuss it with your informant. Try to get an understanding of the organizational principles that are used in the plant. If it is part of a larger concern or group, indicate its place in the overall structure. (open question)   200

11 [2.2./2.14] Hierarchical stratification, levels (possibly according to salary levels) **of all employees and supervisors. A supervisor is someone who has at least one subordinate excluding personal secretaries.***

Level	Name	Total number of employees	Number of supervisors
1			
2			
3			
4			
5			
6			
7			
8			

Level	Name	Total number of employees	Number of supervisors
9			
10			
TOTAL	202	201	203

---

* CODING INSTRUCTION:

code only:

- total number of employees (VAR 201)
- total number of levels (VAR 202)
- total number of supervisors (VAR 203)

---

12 **What are your present work schedules**
(official working time, shift system etc.;
obtain a full picture for later coding):

---

13 **Have work rosters changed over the period
of the last ten years?** ☐ yes ☐ no

**14 [2.3] How do you group the people at each
hierarchical level into the 'PO' categories?**

	1975/76	1983	1984	current	Total
D Top management (of the Establishment)					$T_D = 207$
C Middle management					$T_C = 206$
B First line supervisors					$T_B = 205$
A Workers					$T_A = 204$
TOTAL	%	(% ♀)	(% ♀)	(% ♀)	TOT =

—% ♂

—TOTAL 1980 ♂ ♀

If possible probe for details.

---

15 **If personnel was reduced in the past 10 years, how
was this accomplished:**

(a) natural wastage and attrition
(b) dismissal (% worker level)
(c) combination of (a) and (b)

16 **Has over the period of last ten years *part-time work***
(a) remained the same
(b) increased
(c) decreased
(d) not applicable

17 **Do you presently have/have you had during the last 12 months *short time work*** ☐ yes ☐ no

18 **How about the last ten years, short time work**
(a) remained the same
(b) increased
(c) decreased
(d) not applicable

19 [2.10] **Would you give the number of *distinguishable* units, sub units, function and staff units according to the following categories?**
(1) PRODUCTION—number of units—names of units: 216
(2) ADMINISTRATION + PERSONNEL—number of units—names of units: 217
(3) TECHNICAL—number of units—names of units: 218
(4) SALES + MARKETING, PURCHASING, STORES—number of units—names of units: 219
(5) FINANCE + ACCOUNTING—number of units—names of units: 220

20 [2.11] **Which of the following specialized functions are present in this organization?**
(A function is specialized when at least one person performs that function and no other function. No account is taken of either (a) the specialist's status or (b) whether an organization has many specialists or only one.)
1. Public relations and advertising 221–236
2. Sales and services
3. Transport
4. Employment
5. Training
6. Welfare and security
7. Buying and stock control

8. Maintenance
9. Accounts
10. Production control
11. Inspection
12. Methods such as work study, OR, rate fixing, etc.
13. Design and development
14. Organization and methods
15. Legal
16. Market research

....

21 [2.12] Formalization of Role Definition

The degree of formalization of role definition in the organization is given by the number of specific role-defining documents—from a set list—which exist in the organization, and, in some cases, the extent of their application or distribution.

(1) Information booklets on general
information/overview of the firm, etc.   237

	Score
None	1
Few employees	2
Many employees	3
All employees	4

(3) Organization chart given to: 238

None	1
Chief executive only	2
Chief executive plus one other executive	3
All/most department heads	4
Most of employees	5

Do the following documents exist?   239

	No	Yes
(4) Written detailed work instructions	1	2
(5) Written terms of reference or job description:		
(a) for direct workers	1	2
(b) for line superordinates	1	2
(c) for staff other than line superordinates	1	2
(d) for chief executive	1	2
(6) Work routines and administrative practices	1	2
(7) Written policies (e.g. personnel policies, etc.)	1	2
(8) Work-flow (production) schedule or programme	1	2

(9) Written research programme or reports 247

....

22 [2.13] If detailed Organization Chart is available, please derive the following data:

    (1) *Chief executive's span of control*: number of subordinates reporting directly with no intervening level, whatever their job or status (excluding personal secretaries).   248

    (2) *Vertical span*: number of posts between direct worker and chief executive of the unit of organization (excluding deputies to, assistants to, and secretaries), in the longest 'line'.   249

§3 Personnel Policy

....

23 [3.0] Introductory question: Please describe this plant's policy or philosophy regarding the personnel. (open question)   300

....

24   How easy or difficult is it to fill each vacancy for a

	very easy	easy	difficult	very difficult
skilled worker				
semi-skilled worker				
unskilled worker				

....

25   How easy or difficult is it to find an equivalent job in their area (money- and competence-wise) **for a**

	very easy	easy	difficult	very difficult
skilled worker				
semi-skilled worker				
unskilled worker				

....

26 [2.4] Foreign workers, total number (currently)   ☐

....

27 [2.6] Professional differentiation of (level A/P) **workers**

skilled personnel ☐   317

semi-skilled ☐   318

unskilled ☐   319

28 Has over the period of the past ten years the need of training of your employees in your firm (in order to meet the skill requirements)

increased ☐3

remained the same ☐2

lessened ☐1

If ☐3 in what fields?

29 [2.7] Work days per year (man-days* or equivalent units used)

	Total	Production workers (A/P)	White collar workers (A/A)
Total work days scheduled	320	324	328
Total work days lost because of absenteeism	321	325	329
Total work days lost because of accidents	322	326	330
Total work days lost because of strikes	323	327	331

30 [2.8] Number of persons that have left on their own decision during last (1984/85) **year.**

Total	Production workers (A/P)	White collar workers (A/A)
332	333	334

* given in absolute numbers

§4. Economic And Financial Data
VAR 700–824

....

31 [4.2] Ownership

(1) Legal status of the firm   400

(2) Any change in legal status during last ten years?
    If yes—why   401

(3) Total number of voteholders   ☐   402

(4) Directors (percentage of equity owned by all
    directors or top supervisory board)   ☐   403

(5) Number of directors who are executives   ☐   404

(6) When was the company established?   ☐   405

(7) Are directors founders of the firm?   ☐   406

                                        No   1

                                      Some   2

                                       All   3

(8) Do any external financial groups (beside the
    owners) have an influence on this company?   407

                   Yes, very strong influence   1

                       Yes, limited influence   2

                               No influence   3

(9) Dependency on large company (ask name)   408

   (1) Size of unit as % of size (number of employees)
       of total parent organization

   (2) Have there been any recent changes in
       dependency (ownership)   409

                                       Yes   2

                                        No   1

   (3) Public accountability of company   410

                                       Yes   2

                                        No   1

(10) Status of Organization unit within large
     company: 411

        Branch   1

        Head Branch (headquarters on same location) 2

        Subsidiary (legal identity)   3

        Principal unit   4

(11) Unit representation on policy-making bodies: 412

Unit not represented on top-policy-making body   = 1
Unit represented on local policy-making body but
not on top-policy-making body   = 2
Unit represented on policy-making body   = 3

32 [4.3] Dependency on other power groups

(1) % of directors on top supervisory boards beyond
this organization   □   413

Dependency on consumers

(2) a. Response of outputs volume to customer
influence   414

Stock mainly	1
Stock and order	2
Order mainly	3

   b. Main type of link with customers   415

Single orders	1
Short term/subcontract	2
Long term contracts	3
Ownership (internal exchange)	4

   c. Dependence of organization on its largest
costumer   416

Minor outlet (less than 10% of output)	1
Medium outlet (over 10% of output)	2
Major outlet (over 50% of output)	3
Sole outlet	4

Environmental change

(3) How often does each of the following factors change?   424

	never	almost never	sometimes	frequently	very often
Consumers					
a. The distributors of your product	1	2	3	4	5
b. The actual users	1	2	3	4	5
Supply					
c. Suppliers of new materials	1	2	3	4	5
d. Suppliers of equipment	1	2	3	4	5
e. Suppliers of product parts	1	2	3	4	5
f. Supply of labor	1	2	3	4	5

	never	almost never	sometimes	frequently	very often
Competition					
g. Competition for suppliers	1	2	3	4	5
h. Competition for costumers	1	2	3	4	5
Socio-political position					
i. Government control over your industry	1	2	3	4	5
j. Public political attitude towards industry and its particular product	1	2	3	4	5
k. Relationships with trade unions	1	2	3	4	5
Technology					
l. Technological requirements in own and related industries	1	2	3	4	5
m. Improvement and development of new products	1	2	3	4	5

33 [4.4] MARKET SITUATION

	low	moderate	high	%
(1) Degree of competition in this industry/line of business	1	2	3	43
(2) Market share (%) in this country	1	2	3	43 3
(3) Sales (%) exported to other countries	1	2	3	43 3
(6) This plant's dominance in its industry	1	2	3	43

What stage of the trade-cycle exists presently for
(as seen by interviewee)

(8) industry (or country) as a whole

growth	stagnation	recession	depression	revival	43
1	2	3	4	5	

(9) this industrial sector (or line of business)

growth	stagnation	recession	depression	revival	43
1	2	3	4	5	

(10) How sensitive is this firm for changes of the trade cycle?

very sensitive		neither nor		insensitive	43
1	2	3	4	5	

34   Industrial Relations variables

Is the company now unionized?

Yes ☐
No ☐
Partly ☐

Has unionization changed over last 10 years?
Yes?—When?—At what level in organization?

Current union strength
% of manual labour (blue collar)
% of clerical or white collar (excluding management)
% of foremen and management
Overall unionization of plant, currently
How many shop stewards are currently operating?
How many full time? Part time?

Instruction

Only to be filled out by the Top
management

---

§5. Top Management—Interview Guide

35 [5.0] Strategy

(a) What critical events have been registered over
the last ten years?

(b) Would you discuss some of the strategic policies
for the development of the company in the last
10 years? Still same today?

(c) Which function would you consider was of
strategic importance to the company during the
last 10 years? How does this look now?

Managerial Ideology

36 [5.4] What is the self-concept of the top management?

- role within the firm e.g. entrepreneur/ manager/administrator/facilitator, controller, etc.
- role *vis-à-vis* personnel in general, e.g. leadership, direct participation of employees, involvement

37 [5.5] Attitudes
(it seems important to obtain management's perceptions as to what is likely to happen and how they evaluate the forecasts)

- regarding fringe benefits
- regarding unions
- regarding employers' association
- regarding local politics
- regarding the general economic situation

Instruction

Administer the attached questionnaire to your top-management informant(s)

---

38   To be asked of member of top management only:

We would like you to judge the performance of your organization relative to other organizations. Consider separately each of the following characteristics:

profitability, efficiency, growth, morale, adaptability

For each characteristic, indicate your answer by putting a tick in one of the divisions of the scale.

6.1	very profitable			average			not very profitable	439
	1	2	3	4	5	6	7	

6.2	very efficient			average			not very efficient	440
	1	2	3	4	5	6	7	

6.3	high rate of growth			average			low rate of growth	441
	1	2	3	4	5	6	7	

6.4	high morale			average			low morale	442
	1	2	3	4	5	6	7	

6.5	very adaptable (to market)			average			not very adaptable	443
	1	2	3	4	5	6	7	

6.6	very adaptable (in technology)			average			not very adaptable	444
	1	2	3	4	5	6	7	

6.7	very adaptable (in personnel policy)			average			not very adaptable	445
	1	2	3	4	5	6	7	

	A		B		C		D		E		F		G	
	Basis	Mode	Basis	Mode	Basis	Mode	Basis	Mode	Basis	Mode	Basis	Mode	Basis	Mode
1 Improvements in work conditions of a work group on workers' level (dust, noise, safety),														
2 Appointment of a new department head														

Instruction

Add all other decisions up to # 18, see PO1

References

Albeda, W. (1984), 'European Industrial Relations in a Time of Crisis', in P. Drenth,*et al.* (eds.), *Handbook of Work and Organisational Psychology.* (Chichester: John Wiley & Sons): ii. 1145–63.

—— (1987), Albeda (1984) was reprinted in 1987

Baglioni, G., and Crouch, C. (eds.) (1990), *European Industrial Relations: The Challenge of Flexibility* (London: Sage).

Bamber, G., and Snape, E. (1987), 'British Industrial Relations', in G. Bamber and R. Landsbury (eds.), *International and Comparative Industrial Relations* (Sydney: Allen & Unwin): 33–56.

Batstone, E. (1988), *The Reform of Workplace Industrial Relations* (Oxford: Clarendon Press).

—— and Gourlay, S. (1986), *Unions, Employment and Innovation* (Oxford: Blackwell).

Beaupain, T. (1987), 'Social Consensus and Industrial Relations in Belgium: From Free Collective Bargaining to Governmental Intervention', paper prepared for the Second European Congress of Industrial Relations, (Tel Aviv).

Blanpain, R. (1983), 'New Technologies and Labour Relations in Belgium', *Bulletin of Comparative Labour Relations*, 12: 159–74).

Blum, A. (1981), *International Handbook of Industrial Relations* (Westport, Conn.: Greenwood Press).

Brown, W. A. (1983), 'Britain's Unions: New Pressures and Shifting Loyalities', *Personnel Management*, 10: 48–51.

Bulletin of the European Communities (00001975), Supplement 8. (Luxemburg: Office for Official Publication of the European Communities).

Bundesanstalt für Arbeit (1987), *Beschäftigungspolitik, Sozial-Versicherungsbeschäftigte am 31.3.87* (Nuremberg: BAA).

Cole, R. (1979), *Work, Mobility and Participation* (Berkeley, Calif.: Univ. of California Press).

Commision of the European Communities (1983), *New Technology and Changes in Industrial Relations: An Anglo-Saxon Comparison* (Vols. Doc 509–83-EN). (Brussels).

Crouch, C., and Heller, F. (eds.) (1979), *International Yearbook of Organisational Democracy*, i (Chichester: John Wiley & Sons).

Crozier, M. (1964), *The Bureaucratic Phenomenon* (Chicago: University of Chicago Press).

Daniel, W. W. (1987), *Workplace, Industrial Relations and Technical Change* (London: Pinter and Policy Studies Institute).

Di Martino, V. (1987), 'Social Dialogue and New Technologies in Europe: The Attitudes of the Parties Involved', Paper prepared for the Second European Congress of Industrial Relations (Tel Aviv).

DIO (Decisions in Organisations) (1979), 'Participative Decision-Making: A Comparative Study', *Industrial Relations*, 18: 295–309.

Dirrheimer, A., and Wilpert, B. (1983), *Einführung neuer Informationstechnik: Fallstudien zur Kooperation von Management, Betriebsräten und Mitarbeitern* (Technische Universität Berlin: Institut für Psychologie).

Dostal, W. (1982), 5 Jahre Mikro-Elektronik-Diskussion, *Mitteilungen aus der Arbeitsmarkt-und Berufsforschung*, 151–66.

Drenth, P. J. D., and Wilpert, B. (1980), 'The Role of "Social Contracts" in Cross-Cultural Research', *International Review of Applied Psychology*, 29: 293–305.

Dryll, J. (1987), 'Only or as much as?', *Zycie Gospodarcze*, 43: 2.

Edwards, P. K., and Sisson, K. (1989), 'Industrial Relations in the UK: Change in the 1980s', *IRRU* (University of Warwick).

Elvander, N. (1987), 'Can the Government Control Wage Negotiations?' paper presented at the Second Regional Congress of Industrial Relations (Tel Aviv).

Foundation for the Improvement of Living and Working Conditions (1989), *New Information Technology and Participation in Europe* (Dublin: Loughlinstown House).

Fürstenberg, F. (1987), 'Industrial Relations in the Federal Republic of Germany', in G. J. Bamber and R. D. Landsbury (eds.), *International and Comparative Industrial Relations* (Sydney: Allen & Unwin).

Gevers, P. (1987), 'The Trade Union Movement and the System of Industrial Relations in Belgium', paper presented at the Second European Regional Congress on Industrial Relations (Tel Aviv).

Gilejko, L. (1987), 'Workers' Council in Action', paper presented at a seminar at the Central Commitee of the Polish United Workers Party (Warsaw).

Gouldner, A. (1954), *Patterns of Industrial Bureaucracy* (New York: The Free Press).

Grela, L. (1987), 'Workers' Self-Management and Collective Forms of Work', *Nowe Drogi*, 8: 26.

Guest, D., and Peccei, R. (1992), 'Employee Involvement: Redundancy as a Critical Case', *Human Resource Management Journal*, 2: 34–59.

Gustavsen, B. (1983), 'The Norwegian Work Environment Reform: The Transition from General Principles to Workplace Action', in C. Crouch and F. Heller (eds.), *Organisational Democracy and Political Processes* (Chichester: John Wiley & Sons): 545–63.

—— and Hunnius, G. (1981), *New Patterns of Work Reform: The Case of Norway* (Oslo and New York: Oslo Univ. Press and Columbia Univ. Press).

Haas, P. (1983), 'The Aftermath of Sweden's Co-determination Law: Workers' Experience in Gothenbur 1977–1980', *Economic and Industrial Democracy*, 4/1: 19–46.

Hammarstrom, O. (1987), 'Swedish Industrial Relations', in G. Bamber and R. Landsbury (eds.), *International and Comparative Industrial Relations* (Sydney: Allen & Unwin): 187–227.

Hanami, T., and Monat, J. (1988), 'Employee Participation in the Workshop in the Office and in the Enterprise', in E. Blanpain (ed.), *Comparative Labour Law and Industrial Relations* (Deventer: Kluwer): 249–86.

Hansen, E. J. (1986), *Danskermes Levekar 1986, Samnenboldt Med 1976* (Copenhagen).

Heller, F. A. (1984), 'The Role of Longitudinal Method in Management Decision-making', in James G. Hunt, Dian-Marie Hosking, C. Schriesheim, and Rosemary Stewart (eds.), *Leaders and Managers: International Perspectives on Managerial Behaviour and Leadership* (New York: Pergamon Press).

—— and Drenth, P. J. D., Koopman, P., and Rus, V. (1988), *Decisions in Organisations: A Three-Country Longitudinal Study* (London: Sage).

IDE (1981a), *European Industrial Relations* (Oxford: Clarendon Press).

—— (1981b), *Industrial Democracy in Europe* (Oxford: Oxford Univ. Press).

Inglehart, R. (1977), *The Silent Revolution* (Princeton, NJ: Princeton Univ. Press).

Institut Syndical Européen (1980), *Nouvelles formes d'organization du travail: les experiences en europe occidentale* (Brussels).

Jain, H., Vanachter, O., and Gevers, P. (1980), 'Success and Problems with Participative Schemes: The Case of Belgium', in H. Jain (ed.), *Worker Participation Success and Problems* (New York: Praeger): 105–126.

Kassalow, E. (1987), 'Trade Unions and Industrial Relations: Toward the Twenty-First Century', *Bulletin of Comparative Labour*, 16: 1–25.

Kauppinen, T. (1987), *Labour Relations in Finland* (Helsinki: Government Printing Centre).

Kelly, J., and Richardson, R. (1989), Annual Review Article, 1988, *British Journal of Industrial Relations*, 27/1.

Kern, H., and Schumann, M. (1984), *Das Ende der Arbeitsteilung? Rationalisierung in der industriellen Produktion: Bestandaufnahme, Trendbestimmung* (Munich: Beck).

Kochan, T. A., Katz, H., and McKersie, R. B. (1986), *The Transformation of American Industrial Relations* (New York: Basic Books).

Krawczyk, R. (1981), *Reforma gospodarcza (Economic Reform: Proposals, Tendencies, Directions of Discussions, Selected Documents)* (Warsaw: Paristwowe Wydan, Ekonomiczne).

Lafferty, W. M. (1984), 'Workplace Democratization in Norway: Current Status and Future Prospects with Special Emphasis on the Role of the Public Sector', *Acta Sociologica*, 27: 123–38.

—— (1988), *Political Change in Norway* (Institute of Political Science, University of Oslo).

—— (1990), 'The Political Transformation of a Social Democratic State', *West European Politics*, 13/1: 79–100.

Lammers, C., and Szell, G. (1989), *International Handbook of Participation in Organizations*, i (Oxford: Oxford Univ. Press).

Lawler, E. E. (1986), *High Involvement Management: Participative Strategies for Improving Organizational Performance* (San Francisco: Jossey-Bass).

Laydall, H. (1989), *Yugoslavia in Crisis* (Oxford: Oxford Univ. Press).

Lind, J. (1988), *Labour Market Policy and Industrial Relations in Denmark* (Aalborg: ATA-Projektet).

Long, R. J. (1986), 'Recent Patterns of Swedish Industrial Democracy', in R. Stem and S. McCarty (eds.), *The Organizational Practice of Democracy* (Chichester: John Wiley & Sons): 375–86.

—— and Warner, M. (1984), 'Organizations, Participation and Recession: A Critical Analysis of Changes in the Pattern of Employee Involvement over the Last Decade'. Unpub. MS.

—— and —— (1987), Organizations, Participation and Recession: An Analysis of Recent Evidence, *Relations Industrielles*, 42/1: 65–91.

Martin, A. (1987), 'The End of the Swedish Model? Recent Developments in Swedish Industrial Relations', in E. Kassalow (ed.), *Unions and Industrial Relations* (Antwerp: Kluwer): 93–127.

Millward, N., and Stevens, M. (1986), *British Workplace Industrial Relations, 1980– 1984* (Aldershot: Gower).

Mintzberg, H. (1983), *Structure in Fives: Designing Effective Organizations* (London: Prentice Hall International).

Monat, J., and Sarfati (1986), *Workers' Participation: A Voice in Decisions* (Geneva: ILO).

Okubayashi, K. (1989), 'The Japanese Industrial Relations System', *Journal of General Management*, 14/3: 67–88.

Pasić, N., Grozdanić, S., and Radević, M. (1982), *Workers' Management in Yugoslavia* (Geneva: ILO).

Peretiatkowicz, A. (1989), 'Democracy in Selected Polish State Enterprises', *Economic Analysis and Workers' Management*, 23: 31–42.

Pipkon, J. (1984), 'Employee Participation in the European Community: Progress and Pitfalls', in B. Wilpert and A. Sorge (eds.), *International Perspectives on Organizational Democracy* (Chichester: John Wiley & Sons): 49–70.

Pool, J., Drenth, P. J. D., Koopman, P. L., and Lammers, C. J. (1988), De volwassenwording van medezeggenschap. *Gedrag en Organisatie*, 1/3, 37–58.

—— and Koopman, P. L. and Mijs, A. A. (forthcoming), De medezeggenschap na tien jaar no-nonsense management. *Tijdschrift voor Arbeidsmaagstukken*.

Pugh, D. S., and Hickson, D. J. (1976), *Organizational Structure in its Context: The Aston Programme I* (Farnborough: Saxon House).

Ramondt, J. (1987), 'Managing Dualism in Dutch Employees', *International Studies of Management and Organizations*, 17/2, 78–85.

Roberts, B. C. (1985), 'Great Britain', in B. C. Roberts (ed.), *Industrial Relations in Europe: The Imparatives of Change* (London: Croom Helm): 100–36.

Rojot, J. (1987), 'The Attitudes of Employers and Trade Unions Towards the Quality of Working Life Movement', in R. Blanpain (ed.), *Comparative Labour Law and Industrial Relations* (Deventer: Kluwer): 307–36.

—— (1989), 'Structural Change and Industrial Relations Strategies in 8th World Congress', *Structural Change and Industrial Relations Strategies* (Brussels: International Industrial Relations Association): 1–16.

Ramsey, H. (1983), 'Evolution or Cycle? Worker Participation in the 1970s and 1980s', in C. Crouch and F. A. Heller (eds.), *International Yearbook of Organisational Democracy* (Chichester: John Wiley & Sons): 203–25.

Rosenstein, E. (1989), 'Quality of Working Life: Background, Contents and Dilemmas as Seen From a Western Perspective', *Hitotsubashi Journal of Social Studies*, 21/1: 89–104.

—— Ofek, A., and Harel, G. (1987), 'Organizational Democracy and Management in Israel', *International Studies of Management and Organization*, 17/2: 52–68.

Russell, R., and Rus, V. (1991), *International Handbook of Participation in Organizations*, ii (Oxford: Oxford Univ. Press).

Sandberg, A. (1984), *Technological Change and Co- determination in Sweden* (Stockholm: Aarbetslivcentrum).

Schaie, W. K., and Hertzog, C. (1982), 'Longitudinal Methods', in B. B. Woldman (ed.), *Handbook of Developmental Psychology* (New York: Prentice Hall): 91–115.

Stem, R. (1988), 'Participation by Representation', *Work and Occupations*, 15: 396–422.

Stern, R. N., and McCarthy, S. (1986), *International Yearbook of Organizational Democracy*, iii (Chichester: John Wiley & Sons).

Stooß, F. (1985), 'Verliert der "Beruf" seine Leitfunktion für die Integration der Jugend in die Gesellschaft?' *Mitteilungen der Arbeitsmarkt-und Berufsforschung*, 18/2: 198–208.

Streeck, W. (1984), 'Co-determination: The Fourth Decade', in B. Wilpert and A. Sorge (eds.), *International Perspectives on Organisational Democracy* (Chichester: John Wiley & Sons): 391–422.

Suviranata, A. J. (1987), *Labour Law and Industrial Relations in Finland* (Deventer: Kluwer).

Tavitian, R. (1985), 'Trade Union Trends in Western Europe: A European Perspective', in B. C. Roberts (ed.), *Industrial Relations in Europe* (London: Croom Helm): 222–41.

Teulings, A. W. M. (1987), 'A Political Bargaining Theory of Co-determination: An Empirical Test for the Dutch System of Organizational Democracy', *Organizational Studies*, 8/1: 1–24.

Ursell, G. (1983), 'The Views of British Managers and Shop Stewards on Industrial Democracy', in C. Crouch and F. Heller (eds.), *Organisational Democracy and Political Processes* (Chichester: John Wiley & Sons): 327–52.

Wagner, J. A., and Gooding, R. (1987), 'Effects of Societal Trends on Participation Research', *Administrative Science Quarterly*, 32: 241–62.

Wall, T. D., and Lischeron, J. A. (1977), *Worker Participation: A Critique of the Literature and some Fresh Evidence* (London: McGraw Hill).

Warner, M. (1989), 'Human Resources Implication of New Technology', *Human Systems Management*, 6/3: 279–87.

—— (1990), 'Management versus Self-Management in Yugoslavia', *Management Studies*, 1.

Webbs, S. (1989), *Blueprint for Success: A Report on Involving Employees in Britain* (London: Industrial Society Press).

Weiss, M. (1989), 'Structural Change and Relations in the Federal Republic of Germany', International Industrial Relations Association 8th World Congress, September 1989 (Brussels).

Wilpert, B., and Ruiz Quintanilla, S. A. (1984), 'The German Humanization of Work Programme: Review of its first Twenty Publications', *Journal of Occupational Psychology*, 57: 185–95.

—— and Sorge, A. (1984), *International Yearbook of Organizational Democracy*, ii (Chichester: John Wiley & Sons).

List of IDE Publications

Aksnes, K. (1978), *Medlemsinnflytelse og organisasjonstuvikling i samvirkeorganisasjoner i landbrutet*, Institutt for Landbruksökonomi, As, Norway: Norwegian Agriculture University.

Andriessen, Eric J. H. (1976), 'Meer Zeggenschap voor de Nieuwe Ondernemingsrad?' *Intermediair*, 12.

Andriessen, J. H. T. H. (1976), 'The Dutch Industrial Relations System', *Industrial Relations Journal*, 2: 49–59.

—— Drenth, P. J. D., and Lammers, C. J. (1983), *Medezeggenschap in Nederlandse Bedryven* (Amsterdam: KOW. AC. v. Wetensch).

Belgian IDE Team (1978), *(IDE) Belgian Report 1*, Rapporten van het Laboratorium en Seminarie voor Toegepaste Psychologie (Ghent: Rijksuniversiteit Gent, 1).

Belgian ZIDE Team (1979–80), *Organisatiestructuur en organisatieontwikkeling in ziekenhuizen. Intraziekenhuizenrapport*, Rapporten van het Laboratorium en Seminarie voor Toegepaste Psychologie (Ghent: Rijksuniversiteit Gent, 7A-Q).

Bengtsson (n.d.). *LOs ach TCOs inställning i personalpolitiska fragor under 1960-och 1970-talen* (Uppsala: Department of Business Administration).

Björklung, L. (1977), *Upplevt inflytande och önskad förändering hos arbetare vig tre metallindustrier* (Uppsala: Department of Business Administration).

Claes, R., and Frees, P. (1991), *Industrielle democratie in Vlaanderen. Evolutie van 1976 naar 1986*, Rapporten van het Seminarie en Laboratorium voor Sociopsychologie van het Bedrijfsleven en voor Testontwikkeling (Ghent: Rijksuniversiteit Gent, 2).

Coetsier, P. (1978), 'Een heel stuk blijft buiten de OR', *100 jaar Personeelsvertegenwoordiging*, KNG & SF: Delft, 10–11.

—— and Ryckaert, M. (1978), *(IDE) The Belgian Industrial Relations System*, Rapporten van het Laboratorium en Seminarie voor Toegepaste Psychologie (Ghent: Rijksuniversiteit Gent, 2).

—— and Andriessen, E. (1982), 'Bedrijfsdemocratisering', in P. Drenth, *et al.* (ed.), *Handboek of Arbeids-en Organisatiepsychologie* (Deventer: Van Loghum Slaterus).

—— —— (1984), 'Industrial Democratization', in P. Drenth, *et al.* (ed.), *Handbook of Work and Organizational Psychology* (Chichester: John Wiley & Sons).

—— and Claes, R. (1983), 'Beleidsvorming en machtsverdeling in ziekenhuizen', *Hospitalia*, 1: 16–25.

—— —— (1987), *(IDE) Replicatiestudie 76–86*, Rapporten van het Laboratorium en Seminarie voor Toegepaste Psychologie (Ghent: Rijksuniversiteit Gent, 45).

—— —— (1988), 'Organisation and Participation in Belgian Hospitals', in D. Wallis and C. de Wolff (eds.), *Stress and Organisational Problems in Hospitals* (London: Crook Helm): 241–66.

—— —— Vrij, M., and Claeys, P. (1980), *Organisatiestructuur en organisatieontwikkeling in ziekenhuizen*, Rapporten van het Laboratorium en Seminarie voor Toegepaste Psychologie (Ghent: Rijksuniversiteit Gent, 9).

—— and Ryckaert, M. (1978*a*), *(IDE) Eerste Belgische resultaten in het Europees onderzoek naar de effecten van participatiestructuren*, Rapporten van het Laboratorium en Seminarie voor Toegepaste Psychologie (Ghent: Rijksuniversiteit Gent, 3).

—— —— (1978*b*), *(IDE) The Belgian Industrial Relations System*, Rapporten van het Laboratorium en Seminarie voor Toegepaste Psychologie (Ghent: Rijksuniversiteit Gent, 2, 34).

—— —— (1980), *(IDE) Belgisch Eindrapport*, Rapporten van het Laboratorium en Seminarie voor Toegepaste Psychologie (Ghent: Rijksuniversiteit Gent, 6, 100).

DeCorte, W. (1979), 'Realiteitswaarde van de notie feitelyke participatie: en studie in de variate taal van het sociopsychologisch onderzoek', *Psychologica Belgica*, 19: 330–60.

Dreisler, P. (1976), 'Måling af magt', *Organisatoriske Fragmenter*, 1–16.

—— (1978), 'Indflydelsesforgeling i danske virksomheder—om IDE-undersøgelsens gennemforelske i Danmark', *Organisatoriske Fragmenter*, 1–24.

—— (1979*a*), 'Delegering—demokratisering, nogle resultater fra en undersøgelse', in Ingolf Stahl (ed.), *Forskning—utbildning—praxis* (Stockholm: Handelshögskolan i Stockholm): 15.

—— (1979*b*), 'Industrial Democracy—The Danish Case', *Organisatoriske Fragmenter*, 1–22.

—— (1979*c*). 'Participation på europæiske arbejdspladser', *Organisatoriske Fragmenter*, 1–20.

—— (1979*d*). 'Selvforvaltning—Hvad er det?', *Organisatoriske Fragmenter*, 1–15.

—— (1980*a*), 'A Comparison of Own Perceived Participation and Two Measures of Rated Influence in the Project "Distribution of Power and Influence in Danish Companies" ', *Organisatoriske Fragmenter*, 1–22.

—— (1980*b*), 'The Locomotive of Influence', *Organisatoriske Fragmenter*, 1–18.

Drenth, P. J. D. (1981), *Cross Cultural Organisational Psychology: Challenges and Limitations*, in S. H. Irvine and J. Berry, *Human Assessment and Cultural Factors* (London: Plenum Press): 563–80.

—— and Wilpert, B. (1980), 'The Role of "Social Contracts" in Cross-cultural Research', *International Review of Applied Psychology*, 29: 293–305.

Goetschy, J. (1981*a*), 'Participation et pouvoir dans l'enterprise: Étude des stratégies et des représentations' (thesis, Paris: Institut d'Études Politiques).

—— (1981*b*), 'Les Théories du pouvoir', *Sociologie du Travail*, 447–68.

Heller, Frank A., Wilders, Malcolm, Abell, Peter, and Warner, Malcolm (1979), *What do the British want from Participation and Industrial Democracy?* (London: Anglo-German Foundation for the Study of Industrial Society).

Industrial Democracy in Europe (IDE) (1976), 'Industrial Democracy in Europe: An International Comparative Study', *Social Science Information*, 15: 173–203.

—— (1979), 'Participation: Formal Rules, Influence and Involvement', *Industrial Relations*, 18/3: 273–94.

—— (1980), 'Die Messung von Mitbestimmungsnormen—Darstellung eines international vergleichenden Forschungsansatzes', in E. Blankenburg and K. Lenk (eds.), *Jahrbuch der Rechtssoziologie und Rechtstheorie*, vii (Opladen: Westdeutscher Verlag).

—— (1981*a*), *European Industrial Relations* (Oxford: Oxford Univ. Press).

Industrial Democracy in Europe (IDE) (1981*b*), 'Industrial Democracy in Europe: Differences and Similarities across Countries and Hierarchies', *Organization Studies*, 2/2: 113–29.

—— (1981*c*), *Industrial Democracy in Europe* (Oxford: Oxford Univ. Press).

—— (1981*d*), 'The Role of Formal Norms in the Introduction of Industrial Democracy', *Economic Analysis and Workers' Management*, 351–61.

Laaksonen, Oiva, Kauhanen, Juhani, Kivisaari, Sirkku, and Vanhala, Sinikka (1979), *Päätöksentekoon Osallistuminen, arvot ja tyytyväisyys yrityksissä* (Helsinki: Helsingin Kauppakorkeakoulun Julkaisuja).

Lethinen, H. (1979), *Viralliset osallistumisjärjesteemät Suomessa, Routsissa, Englannissa ja Saksan Liittotasavallassa* (Helsinki: Helsingin Kauppakorkeakoulun Julkaisuja).

Martin, D. (1981), 'Réflexions sur la participation', *Revue française des affaires sociales*, 3.

—— and Goetschy, J. (1980), *Participation et pouvoir dans l'enterprise* (Paris: CRESST).

—— and Dupuy, François (1977), *Les Jeux et enjeux de la participation* (Paris: CRESST).

Meurs, P., Claes, R., Lammers, C., and Coetsier, P. (1987), 'Medezeggenschap in ziekenhuizen: Nederland en Vlaanderen vergeleken', *Tijdschrift voor Arbeidsvraagstukken*, 4: 28–36.

Pettersson, B. (1978), *Beslutssituationer i företag—arbetsrättsliga aspekter* (Uppsala: Department of Law).

Piili, M. (1978), *Henkilöstön osallistuminen päätösentekoon yrityksissä*. Helsinki: Helsingin Kauppakoreakoulun Julkaisuja).

Pusić, V. (1977), *Samoupravljanje i industrijska demokracija u Evropi, i* (Ljubljana: Institut za Sociologiju).

—— and Rus, V. (1978), *Samoupravljanje i industrijska demokracija u Evropi, ii* (Ljubljana: Institut za Sociologiju).

Qvale, T. U. (1978), *Induviduell medvirkning eller kollektiv innflytelse i arbeidslivet. Oppsummering av endel hovedresultater fra studien: Industrial Democracy in Europe* (Oslo: Work Research Institutes).

—— (1979), 'Industrielt demokrati—Induviduell medvirkning eller kollektiv innflytelse?' *Bedriftsutvalgene* (Oslo), 1: 2–14.

Rayley, Jörg (1979), *Sozialpsychologische Determinanten der Partizipationswünsche von Mitarbeitern in deutschen Unternehmen—eine empirische Untersuchung* (Diplomarbeit Technische Universität Berlin).

—— and Wilpert, B (1982), '(IDE) Ausgewählte Ergebnisse eines 12-Ländervergleichs', in H. G. Nutzinger (ed.), *Mitbestimmung und Arbeitsselbstverwaltung* (Frankfurt and New York: Campus).

Rooj, P. A. de (1980*a*), *Kapitaal en arbeid in de produktiecooperatie*. Unpubl. ms. Free Univ. of Amsterdam.

—— (1980*b*), *Speciale zeggenschapsverhoudingen*. Unpubl. ms. Free Univ. of Amsterdam.

Rus, V. (1984), 'Industrial Relations and Industrial Democracy in Europe', in Hiroshi Yakota (ed.), *Labour Management Mechanisms* Tokyo: Asian Productivity Center.

—— (1986), *Odločanje in moč (Decision-Making and Power)* (Obzorja) Maribor: .

—— and Pusić, V. (1979), *Samoupravljanje i industrijska demokracija u Evropi, iii* (Ljubljana: Institut za Sociologiju).

Sandberg, T. (1979*a*), 'Arbetarnas krav och medbestämmandeavtalen', in Ingolf Stahl (ed.), *Forksning, utbilding, praxis* (Stockholm: School of Economics): i. 82–94.

—— (1979*b*), 'Hur blir medbestämmandet i industriföretagen?' *Economen*, 9: 30–3.

—— Björklund, Lars, and Molin, Roger (1979), *Företags democrati i sex verkstadsföretag* (Lund: Studentlitteratur).

Sario, J. (1979), *Henkilöstön osallistumisjärjestelmä ja osallistumis-halukkuuteen vaikuttavat tekijöt.* Helsinki: Helsingin Kauppakorkeakoulun Julkaisuja).

Schele, J. (1977), *Beslutssituationer i företag—arbetsrättsliga aspekter* (Uppsala: Department of Law).

Stymne, B. A. (1978), 'Inflytandet och arbetstrivseln' in P. Forsblad, S. E. Sjöstrand, and B. A. Stymne (eds.), *Människan i organisationen: Perspektiv på medbestämmande och ledarskap* (Malmö: Liber), 60–71.

—— (1986) 'Industrial Democracy and the Worker', *International Review of Applied Psychology*, 35/1: 101–20.

—— and Kling, M. (1981), Spelet mellan facket och företagsledningen. Sociala strategier för medbestämmande. Malmö: Liber Läromedel, 1–226.

Vadala, T. (1980), 'IDE-La via italiana alla democrazia industriale', *Revue Internationale de Sociologie*.

—— (1981), 'La democrazia industriale in Europa', *Verso l'autogestione*, 3.

Vanhala, S. (1981), *Henkilöstön vaihtoalttiutta säätelevät tekijät yrityksissä*, 51 (Helsinki: Helsingin Kauppakoreakoulun Julkaisuja).

Veium, K. (1978), 'Deltagelse ojg tilfredshet' (thesis, Oslo University: Department of Political Science).

Verdam, J. (1977), 'De control graph, een invloedsmeting nader bekeken'. Unpubl. ms. Free Univ. of Amsterdam.

Westenholz, A. (1978), "*Magt og indflydelse i bestyrelser*", *Nyt fra Samfundsvidenskaberne*. Copenhagen.

Wilpert, B. (1979), 'Meshing Internationality with Interdisciplinarity', in R. Barth and R. Steck (eds.), *Interdisciplinary Research Groups: Their Management and Organization* (Vancouver: International Research Group on Interdisciplinary Programs).

—— (1980), 'Normenstruktur und Partizipationsverhalten in Arbeitsorganisationen', in R. K. Silbereisen (ed.), *Bericht über die 4. Tagung Entwicklungspsychologie* (Berlin: Technische Universität Berlin).

—— (1981), 'Inside Story: Inside IDE', *Organization Studies*, 2/2: 181–4.

—— and Rayley, J. (1978), *A Partial Test of Mulder's Power Distance Reduction Theory*, Referat gehalten auf dem Internationalen Kongreß für Angewandte Psychologie (Munich).

—— —— (1983*a*), 'Nationale Mitbestimmungssysteme und ihre Wirkungen auf Partizipationsverhalten', *Psychologie und Praxis—Arbeits- und Organisationspsychologie*.

—— —— (1983*b*), *Anspruch und Wirklichkeit der Mitbestimmung* (Frankfurt and New York: Campus).

Index of Names

Subject Index